WOMEN OF FAITH®
STUDY GUIDE SERIES

EMBRACING
GOD'S DESIGN
for YOUR LIFE

STUDY GUIDE

SHEILA WALSH

Published by
THOMAS NELSON
Since 1798

www.thomasnelson.com

Published in Nashville, Tennessee, by Thomas Nelson, Inc.

Thomas Nelson, Inc. titles may be purchased in bulk for educational, business, fundraising, or sales promotional use. For information, please email SpecialMarkets@ThomasNelson.com.

ISBN-10: 1-4185-2833-1
ISBN-13: 978-1-4185-2833-1

Printed in China

07 08 09 10 11 MT 5 4 3 2

Contents

A Note to Small Group Leaders

Wonderful things happen when we get together with other women and share our struggles, our joys, our concerns, and our love. We can find people who will believe for us when we are unable to believe in God's love and power. We can have people pray for us when we are unable to pray for ourselves. And we can know God's love as he loves us through our sisters.

To encourage this kind of fellowship and support, we have used a shaded box to highlight several questions in each chapter. These questions lend themselves to group discussion, but—depending on how much time you have together and how well members of your group know one another—you needn't limit yourselves to these questions, and you certainly don't need to try to answer all of them. Pray and ask God to show you what to focus on as you prepare for your small-group time.

A Suggested Structure

Here is one way you could use the hour you have with your small group.

- 5 minutes: Settling in, greeting, and opening prayer. (This will take longer at the first meeting when you'll want to take a few minutes and have people briefly introduce themselves.)

- 30 minutes: Discuss the questions you've chosen to focus on.

- 5 minutes: Invite members to ask any questions that came up as they worked through the study guide but weren't addressed during the discussion time. (If a topic is introduced that can't be adequately covered in this session, plan to address it at the next meeting.)

- 20 minutes: Share prayer requests and pray for one another.

Needless to say, you can spend a little less time in prayer and a little more on discussion—or vice versa. You'll know your group and the people's needs—and you'll have the Holy Spirit to guide you.

AND A FEW MORE TIPS!

Just as I encouraged you to pray before you meet, also pray as you open and close each meeting. And, if someone shares a deep hurt, don't hesitate to put your questions aside and lift her before the Lord's throne of grace.

Don't worry if, after you ask a question, there are moments of silence. Those moments may seem like hours to you, but wait patiently for women to respond. Some may be processing their thoughts, others may be asking the Lord to give them courage to speak, and others may be waiting to let a quieter group member participate. If the silence goes on too long, try rephrasing the question or perhaps offer a brief answer of your own to get the discussion started.

Be sensitive to the different personalities in your group. Some people will have no trouble talking, and some people will not want to say a word. Sit next to the talkative ones. (Not being able to make eye contact with you may keep them quieter!) And sit across from the women who need to be encouraged to speak. Your smile may help draw them out.

Affirm and thank the women who share—whatever they share! Of course, correct any inaccurate understanding of Scripture and any false ideas about God, but be sure to acknowledge with compassion a woman's pain and fear.

Finally, be sure to remind members to keep everything they hear in the group—experiences, prayer requests, worries, fears, anything and everything—confidential. Only then will the group be a safe place for women to share whatever is on their hearts and minds.

As I think about leading a small group, I keep coming back to the Golden Rule. Treat the women in your group the way you would want to be treated—and then watch God do amazing works of healing and transformation in the lives of those wonderful women! And may you be blessed as you are a blessing to them!

The Woman Beneath the Cape

Before we start, I want to know why you picked up this book. What drew you in? Was it the concept? Or maybe the cover or the title? Or did something else get your attention?

- What do you hope to get out of this study?

Let me introduce you to Wonder Woman 1. Her name is "Monica the Magnificent," and she is coming to save the day! Wonder Woman 2 is named "Olivia the Overwhelmed," and she's wondering what day it is!

- Not knowing anything else about Monica and Olivia, with whom do you identify with more? Explain your answer using details from this week or perhaps just the last twenty-four hours.

CAPE AND BOOTS OR CRUMPLED SUITS?

Maybe, like me, you've been both Monica and Olivia (aka "Sheila the Magnificent" and "Sheila the Overwhelmed").

- If you feel this way, what do you think caused you to change from one to the other? And where are you now on the Monica/Olivia spectrum?

Maybe you're not quite feeling wonderfully made these days. I want you to know that God sees you just as you are and loves you just as you are—on crumpled suit days *and* on cape-and-boot days. As you go through this study, you'll come to believe this wonderful truth about wonderful you.

IS THERE A HANDBOOK SOMEWHERE?

- What exactly is expected of us women anyway? What on earth did God have in mind when he created Eve, the very first woman? (Answer those two questions as best you can.)

- In Jeremiah 29:11 the Lord says, "I have good plans for you, not plans to hurt you. I will give you hope and a good future" (NCV). What comfort does this verse offer you today?

- I know that I've been concerned about either missing God's plan or spending so much time trying to figure it out that I miss out on life! What frustration, if any, does the verse stir up in you?

DID THIS THING COME WITH DIRECTIONS?

I am deeply grateful that God is in control of this changing and confusing world. I firmly believe that God is good and we can trust him completely.

Do I hear an "amen"? Or right now are you struggling—and we all do from time to time—to believe that God is in control, that he is good, and that you can trust him completely? If you're struggling, tell him. He already knows you're struggling, and he loves to comfort his struggling children.

At times I've found myself wishing God would let me see his plans. If I knew what was on God's agenda for me, I might find it easier to embrace life whether things are going well or not so well.

- What circumstances or situations come to mind when you read these words?

- What aspects of your life are you finding difficult to embrace? Don't hesitate to talk to God about it.

WARNING SIGNS

Think through these related questions:

- Do you think it would be easier to cope with life's unexpected storms if you had advance warning?

- If you had a picture of how God was going to get you through those storms, do you think you might not lose heart in the middle?

My immediate response to those two questions was a resounding yes! But after I thought about it, I decided I couldn't cope with knowing everything that is to come.

- What stormy event in your life are you glad you didn't know was on its way before it hit? Explain.

- What grace did God provide for you in that situation as you went through it? Be specific—and thankful!

A Personal Letter from God

Imagine being given a letter from God the day you were born. In it he would tell you about the events ahead and, perhaps more important, how to interpret them so that you would make sense of them rather than live according to wrong beliefs, false guilt, or unfounded shame that might grow out of them.

If you sat down today with a sheet of paper and listed some of the events that have most significantly shaped your life, how you see yourself, how you see others, and also explained how you misunderstood what happened to you at key moments, what would you write? (Don't start writing yet. Just start thinking.)

Here are some examples:

My letter to myself would say something like, "When your father struck out in anger, it was not about you. His brain was wounded." "Don't worry about your mom. I am her provider, and I will never fail her." "It doesn't matter what seems to be true or feels true. I am always with you and I love you."

Monica the Magnificent needed to hear: "When your mom and dad divorce, it has nothing to do with you. They both love you just the way you are, good grades and bad. They're broken people."

Olivia the Overwhelmed would like to have known, "Your father's harsh words are simply a recording of what he has heard all his life." "You are full of possibility, and you are beautiful to me."

Did you learn as a child that the way to be loved is to be perfect? Did you grow up in a home where criticism was a daily reality? Are you feeling responsible for your parents' divorce? Are you still longing for the reassurance you never got as a young teenager whose body was changing or not changing in ways you wanted?

- Now it's time to write that note to yourself; address issues like these.

NOT A LETTER BUT A MAP

None of us has the kind of letter you just wrote to yourself, a letter that revealed the truth about the specific questions we struggled with as our lives unfolded. But God did give us a map—his Word—to help us navigate our lives, and we can use it to rebuild our views of ourselves based on what he tells us in those sacred pages.

- Read Psalm 139:13–16. Which phrases are especially significant to you? Memorize them.

God doesn't call any of us to be Wonder Woman, but he does want us to know that he has made us wonderful. His words in Psalm 139, hidden in your heart, can help you believe that more fully.

May the words in this study guide help you identify wrong information you have picked up along the way and exchange it for the life of purpose and wonder to which God has called you. Sections called *A Look in the Mirror* give you the opportunity to pause and reflect on what God has for you in each lesson. The sections called *A Closet Prayer* give you the opportunity to lay before your Father those things you've tried to hide from him, things that the Holy Spirit will uncover. Through all of this, my prayer for you is that God will give you a new vision and a new sense of purpose as his beautiful, beloved, and wonderful child.

Part One

*Surprising Things You Might Find in
Wonder Woman's Closet*

Chapter 1

Insecurity and Low Self-Esteem

INSECURITY: I'VE GOT NOTHING TO WEAR!

America is a couples' culture—and that fact can fuel even Wonder Woman's insecurity at times.

- When has this couples' culture fueled your insecurity?

AN EARLY ENGAGEMENT

After I gave my classmate, Jim, a valentine crafted from a cornflakes box, he gave me a gold band with three sapphires and two diamonds. He'd found it on the beach and, as he explained, had been saving it for the right girl and the right moment. My mother was not pleased with her ten-year-old daughter's engagement—or the ring—and made me turn it in to the police as lost property.

When I was growing up in Scotland, teenagers didn't date much, but I dated even less than most. I was fairly shy and quite uncomfortable with the woman I saw in the mirror.

3

- When you reached dating age, what did you think about the woman you saw in the mirror? What traits did you especially like and/or dislike?

- What people or what events in your life reinforced your feelings—positive or negative—about yourself?

- What individuals or what circumstances in your life—if any—spoke out against your negative feelings about yourself?

NOT SO WONDERFUL

When I was sixteen years old, I was the female lead in the school's production of *West Side Story*. As I sang, "I feel pretty, oh so pretty," a boy stood up and screamed out, "Well, you sure don't look it!" That was one more voice confirming what I already knew: I was not one of the pretty girls.

- What voice or incident in your life has confirmed what you already felt about yourself—that you were not one of the pretty ones?

You Dated Whom?

After college and a broken engagement when I was ten, I decided to concentrate on serving God instead of my love life. Occasionally I would have dinner with someone, but it never came to much. But one date cemented how inadequate I felt as a woman. Yes, this man had dated *the* Wonder Woman, the one with the cape and the boots and the headband. Sigh . . .

That evening after we had dinner, I found myself staring in my bathroom mirror for a long time, plagued with insecurity. *I have nice eyes and a good nose,* I told myself. *I could definitely stand to lose fifteen pounds. My hair is not so much styled as just . . . clean and dry.* The image I saw confirmed what I already knew: Wonder Woman I was not!

- Name one experience with a man that reinforced the feeling that you were inadequate as a woman?

- What images in the media feed a woman's sense of inadequacy?

Ever Been There?

When we compare ourselves to others, we often come up painfully short. One reason is that we too often compare ourselves to our society's unrealistic ideals and to the media's airbrushed images of women. Instead, we need to focus on the wonder of God's plan, his vision for our lives, and the marvelous picture of God's purpose for a woman's life.

> *What would help you focus on God's plan and purpose for your life? Jot down some ideas.*

A Look in the Mirror

> *Why do you think you compare yourself to other women?*

> *How do you honestly believe God sees you? Don't hesitate to read Psalm 139 again!*

A Closet Prayer

These prayers are only suggestions. Pray along with me or feel free to use your own words to share with God what is on your heart.

Father God,

I confess that I don't always like what I see in my mirror. And I compare myself to other women and don't feel as if I am good enough. Help me to know that in you I am more than good enough, that I am loved and treasured.

Amen.

LOW SELF-ESTEEM:
I DON'T LIKE WHAT I SEE IN THE MIRROR

I can only imagine how beautiful Eve must have been. She was God's perfect creation, made in his image. Then she and Adam were banished from the garden—but not before God revealed his plan for the redemption of humankind that would come through Eve's seed. Adam and Eve, though, had no idea how long it would take or what it would cost the Father.

WHAT HAVE WE DONE?

Adam and Eve had never tasted sin, so they did not know what their act of disobedience would cost. Furthermore, in the garden Satan didn't say, "Steal the fruit!" He merely said, "Imagine . . . you could be like God."

- Think about past actions in your own life that you regret. Were those moments presented to you as opportunities for open rebellion? If not, why was—and is—Satan more subtle when he approaches us with an opportunity to sin?

- Did Satan present the consequences when he presented the temptation—or did he simply say, "Imagine . . ."? Explain.

A New Face in the Mirror

The moment Adam and Eve ate the fruit from the forbidden tree, everything changed. That fruit offered knowledge, and once they took a bite, they couldn't give it back. Immediately they *knew* they were naked. For the first time ever, a woman doubted herself and pulled back from God and from her husband and friend. And we have been doing this same thing ever since.

- In what ways do you pull back from God? Why do you do so?

- Why do you put distance between yourself and ones you love?

- In what ways do you try to put on your figurative cape and boots before you approach God? Before you approach people you love?

A WHISPERED PROMISE

Again and again the book of Genesis points to the coming Christ. Consider, for instance, that God rejected the clothes Eve made in an attempt to cover her sin. Instead he provided clothes for her from his own hand, just as he provides us with the righteousness of his only Son to clothe us and cover our sins.

Like Eve, I keep trying to cover my shame. I also keep trying to be good enough for God and for others—and on both counts I always come up short. So, when I couldn't change how I felt about myself inside, I began the punishing pursuit of trying to change the outside.

- In which ways have you tried to cover your shame and change yourself?

New outfits, new hair color, new hairstyles—none of these will ever be enough. That's because the legacy of Eden demands that we, as women, will struggle with what we see reflected in the mirror. And we can choose from among three possible courses of action in response to this struggle:

1. We can bring our low self-esteem to God and ask him to help us.
2. We can blame our feelings on what we are wearing and buy something new.
3. We can do what Adam and Eve did: shift the blame to someone else.

- Which of these options have you tried? Describe the results.

- What, if anything, keeps you from taking your low self-esteem to God and asking for his help?

A Look in the Mirror

Identify one or two ways that Satan subtly tempts you.

What do you use to hide behind when you feel ashamed?

What do you think was Eve's greatest loss? Explain.

A CLOSET PRAYER

Father God,

You know my sin, and you know the ways I have tried to cover myself. I'm realizing that the only effective covering for my shame and low self-esteem is the blood of your Son, Jesus. When I look in the mirror, help me to see what you see—one who is cleansed and forgiven, one who can find a right and healthy sense of self-esteem in your amazing grace and love. In Jesus' name.

Amen.

Chapter 2

Shame and Anger

SHAME: I WILL NEVER BE GOOD ENOUGH!

Shame can be a heavy overcoat that burdens our heart and soul. And shame is the legacy of Eden, which brings us a sense of dread.

SHAME OR GUILT?

Guilt tells me that I've *done* something wrong, but shame tells me that I *am* something wrong.

Several years ago I spoke with the CEO of a large and successful computer software company. Although she had achieved more than she had ever set out to accomplish, she said, "Inside I am miserable. When I was a little girl, my mother told me I was a mistake. I carry that with me to this day. *I am a mistake.*" My heart ached for this woman. Nothing that she had accomplished mattered because she despised who she was. I understand that. Perhaps you do too.

- Do you identify with this woman's feelings? If so, explain why.

- Read Psalm 18:30–32 and Romans 12:2b. Think about God's sovereignty throughout history and in your life. Consider this: Does this God make mistakes? Explain your answer.

- What comfort comes from being reminded—or perhaps told for the first time—that God doesn't make mistakes? What specific situation in your life and/or feelings in your heart does that truth speak to?

It's Not My Fault!

Shame can keep us isolated and lonely. It can make us pull away from others or attack them before they reject us. Blame is often thinly veiled shame.

- Look at Genesis 3:8–13. Who is pointing the finger of blame at whom in this scene? (Hint: There are two pointing and three being pointed at.)

- When God begins speaking to the guilty parties, he first
  addresses the serpent. It is clear that Satan will be our
  enemy all the days that we walk on this earth. But what
  victory does God foretell in Genesis 3:15? (See 1
  Corinthians 15:55–57.)

Next God turns to Eve, and we see that the pain we experience
when giving birth is the result of our sin. However, the gift of life, a
child, is the promise of God. We also learn that the last part of verse
16 can be paraphrased as "You will now have a tendency to dominate your husband, and he will have the tendency to act as a tyrant
over you." Whether it's trying to give directions while your husband
is driving or taking the initiative in spiritual matters, many of us
struggle with a compulsion to control our husbands, which, in turn,
challenges them to reassert their independence.

- When have you seen this battle between the sexes—either
  in your own marriage or someone else's? Give a specific
  example or two.

*Given that, since the Fall, a woman's tendency is
to dominate her husband, what can we women do
to resist that tendency? Write down your thoughts.*

Next, God's solemn words to Adam clearly imply that, before the Fall, work was not a chore, but a joy. God also declares that human beings will taste death rather than live forever.

- As we all know, work is an uphill battle. What does this unavoidable fact suggest about what a wife can do to be a helpmate to her husband?

- What does the inevitability of death mean for the way we live—or ought to live?

The Reality of Shame

Webster's Dictionary defines *shame* as "a painful emotion caused by consciousness of guilt, shortcoming or impropriety." Letting go of this painful emotion, though, is not as easy as letting go of a pencil you're holding in your hand. No matter how many times or in how many ways I tried to get rid of my shame, it found its way back to me until I finally took it to the Cross and let Jesus deal with it.

- What do you understand to be the source of your shame?

- What efforts have you made to "let go" of your shame? What were the results of those efforts?

- Where do you think our shame belongs? Explain.

BORN AGAIN

I gave my life to Christ when I was eleven, but at age thirty-six I realized that I had never given him my shame.

Have you given your life to Christ? If so, reflect on that decision and God's gracious embrace of you as his child. If not, take a moment to read these verses: Romans 3:23; Romans 6:23; and John 3:16. Spend a few minutes being quiet with God. Is he inviting you to acknowledge both your sin and his Son's death on the Cross as punishment for that sin? Do you hear your heavenly Father calling you to accept Jesus as your Savior and Lord and enter into his eternal family? If so, let someone know about your decision.

> *Whether you gave your life to Christ thirty years ago or thirty seconds ago, have you given him your shame? Why or why not? If you haven't, why not do so now? It belongs at the foot of the Cross, and my guess is that—like me—you will never feel more worthless or more loved as you let go of your shame and lay it at Jesus' feet.*

Don't drag your shame with you any longer. Embrace the freeing truth that you are a broken, flawed daughter of Eve but that God loves you as you are and will take your shame from you.

It's important that I note this: I have to keep giving my shame back to God. It's as if shame has a homing device and loves to return to the place it used to rest. I also needed the help of a godly counselor to help me dig up all of shame's roots.

A LOOK IN THE MIRROR

• Write down any ways in which you feel as if you *are* something wrong instead of being someone who has *done* something wrong. Let those ideas become the heart of a prayer in which you release to God your sense of shame.

To what do you trace the roots of your shame? If you're not sure, or if you know but struggle to dig up all its roots on your own, are you open to working with a godly counselor? Why or why not? Know that just as God provides medical doctors for broken bones, he provides godly counselors for broken hearts.

A CLOSET PRAYER

Father God,

At times I feel overwhelmed by shame, so I ask you to help me place this burden at the foot of the Cross. Allow me to put on the garment of forgiveness, grace, love, and acceptance that you have made for me. I ask that you would dress me just as you dressed Eve. In Jesus' name.

Amen.

ANGER: I'M LOSING CONTROL

We don't talk much about anger in the church. In my experience this bears witness to the fact that, like other things we don't talk about (depression, addiction to pornography, sexual abuse), it is a huge problem. My experience has also taught me that anger is often linked to fear and chained to rejection. This is clearly the reality in history's very first family.

ANGER AND REJECTION

Remember how, in Genesis 4:4–6, God rejected Cain's offering and accepted Abel's? God knew the heart of each brother, so he knew Abel gave the very best he had to give, but Cain offered only a token gift.

- What second chance does God give Cain in verse 7?

- What warning does God give at the same time?

- Share a recent example of being at a similar crossroads. Did you choose God's path? If so, why were you able to make that choice? If not, did you see evidence of Satan waiting for you when you gave in to your unbridled emotions? Be specific.

Cain chose the path of emotion and ended up killing his brother, Abel. We are no better than Cain! We kill people with our harsh words, and we kill people by cutting them out of our lives. Anger often fuels such words and decisions.

I was surprised when I realized how much anger I had hidden in my heart. I cannot remember a time in my teenage years when I felt free to express anger, so anger became something that terrified me. I was not equipped to deal with injustice or strong emotion. And I dreaded being out of control.

- Explain in what ways, if any, your experience is similar to mine.

- I also realized that when you suppress an emotion, it's as if you anesthetize your whole heart. What evidence in your life suggests that this has been your experience? When, for instance, have you truly known joy, peace, or contentment?

Anger is part of life. And anger is like fire: when it's used properly, it can be very productive, but if misused, it is deadly. So I have learned to take my anger first and foremost to God. No matter what I am angry about, I let him know everything I'm feeling. Then I ask him for wisdom to keep what would be helpful and productive, and leave with him the stuff that is linked to my pride or hurt feelings. I think of that as *clean* anger. Then I pray for the insight to express what I am feeling in an appropriate way.

- When have you taken your anger to God? How did that prove to be a wise move?

- If you have never been open with God about your anger, what do you think is holding you back? And what could you do to overcome that hurdle?

When we do not acknowledge or deal with our anger, I've found that it leaks out at unexpected moments. Which one of us, for instance, has not wrestled with the knowledge that God is able to answer all our prayers, yet he often doesn't answer the way we want him to? We need to deal with the anger that results from those feelings.

- When has God's answer to a prayer made you angry?

- What did you do with that anger? Did you see it reemerge down the line? Be specific.

Anger is a defense mechanism. It gives us the feeling of control when a situation is beyond our control. But when we push anger under the surface, it will reemerge somewhere down the line. Read on for a case in point.

A Series of Unfortunate Events

Moses was described as "very humble. He was the least proud person on earth" (Numbers 12:3 NCV). But two key moments of anger changed his life forever. The first is recorded in Exodus 2:11–15.

- According to these verses in Exodus 2, what prompted forty-year-old Moses to act in anger?

- What were the consequences of Moses' rash action?

Forty years later, God called Moses to return to the very palace he had run away from and to ask Pharaoh to let his people leave Egypt. After God sent many harsh plagues on the Egyptians, Pharaoh let the Israelites leave, and Moses was their leader. And he led them during their forty-year wandering through the wilderness.

- In Numbers 20:2–12, we see Moses beyond frustrated with the complaining, rebellious Hebrews. What did God instruct Moses to do in order to provide the people with water?

- What did Moses do instead?

- What were the consequences of Moses' rash action?

God told Moses that he would not enter the Promised Land. That may seem a harsh judgment, but what Moses did has great theological and prophetic implications. The rock represented Christ and what he would do on the Cross. Christ was struck "once and for all time" (Hebrews 10:10 NCV). When Moses exploded in rage and struck the rock two and three times, he distorted the prophetic picture of Christ's sacrifice.

- According to Deuteronomy 34:1–6, what tender mercy does God extend to Moses?

- What intimate picture of God's love for Moses do we find in Deuteronomy 34:5–6?

Righteous anger can serve both us and God well. But the right kind of anger is not a quick fuse that blows up in a moment and is out of control. James warns us about that kind of anger: "My dear brothers and sisters, always be willing to listen and slow to speak. Do not become angry easily, because anger will not help you live the right kind of life God wants" (James 1:19–20 NCV).

- Give an example of anger that serves God well.

- Now give an example of anger that serves you and me well.

What can we do to "not become angry easily"?

Encouraged by my counselor to consider why I had hidden anger in my heart for so long, I saw that lurking just under the surface was the real culprit—fear. And we'll get to that in the next session.

A Look in the Mirror

- What specific issues tend to make you angry? Why do you think those are such triggers?

- What do you do when you feel anger beginning to rise up within you?

What would be an appropriate way to deal with that anger?

What are appropriate ways to express anger?

A CLOSET PRAYER

Father God,

I confess that too many times I have let myself become easily angered. And at other times I have held in my anger and it has grown beyond my control. Neither of these is a good, godly, or healthy option. So please help me learn to bring my anger to you to receive grace and mercy. In Jesus' name.

Amen.

Chapter 3

Fear and Masks

FEAR: I'M AFRAID OF WHAT THE FUTURE MIGHT HOLD

It's one thing to watch a scary movie, turn off the television, and know the "bad guy" is no longer a threat. It is quite different when the dark music and scary stranger live in the basement of your soul. Fear can be rooted in a difficult memory that left you with a deep scar or a traumatic event from your past that left a fear of life being out of control once again. Whatever its source, such fear can prompt us to live in the world of *what ifs?*

- What are you afraid of? (Don't let the simplicity of that question leave you satisfied with simplistic answers.)

- What do you tend to do with fear when it arises in your heart?

THE WHAT IFS

Nothing has the ability to conjure up terrible possibilities like our own imagination.

In Philippians 4:6–7, Paul gives us an antidote to our poisonous imaginings: "Do not worry about anything, but pray and ask God for everything you need, always giving thanks. And God's peace, which is so great we cannot understand it, will keep your hearts and minds in Christ Jesus" (NCV).

- When has this practice helped you overcome fear rooted in your own imagination? Give a specific example.

What keeps you from turning to God when you find yourself worrying? What can you do to make turning to God in prayer a more regular, if not automatic, response when you're worried or afraid?

> **Which truths about God's personality quiet your concern about what ifs? See Jeremiah 29:11, Isaiah 43:1–2, and Matthew 28:20b.**

Prayer and peace are God's gifts to us in this world. It's just hard to stay in that peaceful place, isn't it? The *what ifs* began in Eden and have plagued us ever since. Sometimes they are based on our fear of being found out, caught in our sin.

CAUGHT

What if God finds out what we did? Adam had good reason to be afraid, and we see this same fear of being caught in Jacob (When he bestowed his blessing, would Isaac realize that this was Jacob and not Esau?) and in Joseph's brothers (Would Joseph, now a powerful leader in Egypt, recognize the hungry Hebrews as his own brothers, who had sold him into slavery decades earlier?).

- When have you been afraid of being caught in your sin?

- What physical or emotional impact did that fear have on you?

- What did you do in response to that fear? Did you confess your wrongs? Why or why not?

NOT ENOUGH

Sometimes our *what ifs* stem from a fear that we can't do what someone is asking us to do. Our insecurity feeds our belief that we don't have what it takes. Moses felt that way when God called him to be his mouthpiece (Exodus 4:1).

- When have you been suddenly overwhelmed by fear when asked to do something? Were you able to do it? Explain.

- What fear, if any, do you find paralyzing?

I was able to get over my paralyzing fear of public speaking when I found relief in a very simple story about a young boy and his lunch.

THE PACKED LUNCH

Remember when Jesus was teaching a large crowd and noticed how hungry everyone was? He asked his disciples where they could buy enough food for everyone. The men said they'd need to work a month to feed the crowd, but Andrew gave Jesus all he could find—a boy's lunch of five barley loaves and two small fish.

- Read Mark 6:37–44. What did Jesus do when he took in his hands the meager lunch that Andrew offered him?

- After Jesus took the food and blessed it, what miracle did the disciples and the crowd experience?

- What does this scene from Jesus' life call you to do with your worry and fear?

I learned that God asks us to show up with whatever he has packed for us that day and to trust that it will be enough. When you are facing unthinkable circumstances, offer what little faith and courage you have to your Father, and he will make it be enough.

OUT OF CONTROL

Fear can be born out of a very real experience that has left its mark on us.

- What is a recurring fear of yours that developed from a very real experience in your past?

- What impact is that (perhaps) irrational fear having on
  your everyday life and/or important relationships?

Fear can also come from a feeling of helplessness. Often we are terrified of losing control, and that fear drives us to try to grasp control wherever we can.

- In what areas of your life, if any, do you feel helpless?

- What, if anything, do you fear losing control over? Do
  you see yourself trying, as a result, to grasp control? Be
  specific.

For years I thought that if I faced what I was afraid of, it would consume me. But when I brought my fears—of being hurt physically, of making someone angry, of being rejected, of someone I love hurting me—into the light of God's presence, they took on different proportions; they were real and manageable as opposed to the over-exaggerated horrors of what we don't talk about and instead just dread.

- When have you experienced the fact that speaking a fear
  out loud reduces it to a more manageable size?

- What current fear, if any, could you share with a trusted friend or confidant? Do so!

In *Star Wars: Revenge of the Sith*, Yoda said, "The fear of loss is a path to the dark side." Yoda then instructed his listeners to train themselves to let go of everything they were afraid to lose. In contrast, God calls us, his children, to train ourselves by his grace and the power of the Holy Spirit to take all our fears to him. Our worry will not change the future; it will only rob us of joy in the present.

A LOOK IN THE MIRROR

- At the beginning of this chapter, you listed things you are afraid of. What one or two things are you most afraid of? Are you afraid because of *what ifs*, past events, or the desire to be in control?

- What worries—whether they're based on your creative *what ifs* or not—can you lay before God right now? Do so.

- What past events that have caused you to fear will you lay before God right now?

- Finally, does being in control make you feel safer?
  Explain—and talk to God about your battle with fear of
  losing control.

A CLOSET PRAYER

Father,

*I confess that I am sometimes overwhelmed by fear—and I don't
always understand where it is coming from. Teach me to bring
my fears to you. In Jesus' name I pray.*

Amen.

But what if the things we are most afraid of losing are the masks
we wear? We may even have worn them for so long that we don't
know who we are underneath them.

MASKS: I'M AFRAID TO BE SEEN

I love *The Wizard of Oz*. I love the friendship shared between
Dorothy, the Scarecrow, the Tin Man, and the Cowardly Lion. And
I love how their journey to the Emerald City, where they hope to
meet the Great Oz, changes each one of them. The Scarecrow dis-
covers that he has a brain when he uses it to help his friends; the Tin
Man finds out that he is all heart; and the Cowardly Lion finds
courage after all. Each of the four characters who travel down the
Yellow Brick Road is honest and vulnerable with the other three.
They don't hide what they are lacking in their lives. (By the way,
that's how I see our core team at Women of Faith. We each bring
different strengths and struggles to the mix.)

- The Scarecrow didn't have a brain, the Tin Man didn't have a heart, and the Cowardly Lion didn't have courage. What would you say you feel like you're missing?

- Open, transparent friendship helped the Scarecrow discover his brain, the Tin Man his heart, and the Cowardly Lion his courage. As you journey the path of your life, with whom are you able to be open and transparent about your weaknesses and struggles? Let that person—or those people—know how much you appreciate them!

- If your path is lonely, what steps will you take to find friendship and support? Which step will you take this week?

The four friends arrive at the Emerald City still hoping that the wizard will give them all they need to get Dorothy home. But when Dorothy's dog, Toto, pulls back the curtain, the Great Oz is revealed to be a mere man. Similarly, my experience with clinical depression revealed to me that I was a mere woman—not Wonder Woman—and that experience was the means by which God chose to transform me into a very grateful woman who finally understands that she is wonderfully made.

- When has life come crashing down at your feet? Describe the circumstances.

- Describe how you responded—in your head as well as in your heart—to those circumstances.

- As you look back on that season of your life, where do you see God at work? At this point, what can you thank him for?

THE BEGINNING OF THE END

When I was diagnosed with severe clinical depression, I was so ashamed. For years I had found my identity in trying to be the perfect Christian woman. I had worked hard and tried to save myself, but I couldn't. (After all, depression is a very real illness that occurs in the brain when certain chemicals necessary for normal brain function are missing.) Now I was leaving behind everything I had ever counted on to give me my identity—and I was checking myself in as a patient at a psychiatric hospital.

- A key moment in the hospital happened my first morning there. Recognized by another patient, I had to admit that I needed help. To whom have you said—or do you need to say—"I need help"? Do so—and then watch God work!

Another key and God-choreographed moment came when I was going to get my hairdryer one evening. A new patient and her daughters recognized me and began to cry. I learned that night that, when we take off our masks, we can recognize each other's pain.

- When, if ever, has your pain—or another person's pain— served as a bridge between you and another? (If you have seen God use your pain to enable you to help someone who is hurting, know that you will experience this as one way he redeems the pain you suffer.)

When we are willing to stand in our brokenness and let the light of Christ shine through our lives, the good news is preached to the poor in spirit, the blind can see the truth, and the lame and wounded can walk again.

Carefully read though 2 Corinthians 1:3–7 (NCV):

Praise be to the God and Father of our Lord Jesus Christ. God is the Father who is full of mercy and all comfort. He comforts us every time we have trouble, so when others have trouble, we can comfort them with the same comfort God gives us. We share in the many sufferings of Christ. In the same way, much comfort comes to us through Christ. If we have troubles, it is for your comfort and salvation, and if we have comfort, you also have comfort. This helps you to accept patiently the same sufferings we have. Our hope for you is strong, knowing that you share in our sufferings and also in the comfort we receive.

> **What encouragement to be transparent about your**
> **pain do you find in this passage? Underline—**
> **and perhaps even memorize—the key phrases that**
> **speak to you.**

I don't know what masks you are wearing, and I don't know why you feel that you need them. But I do know that if by the grace of God you are able to take them off, you will never pick them up again. Taking off your masks may well cost you, but the overwhelming love of your Father and the companionship of others who have done the same will more than compensate.

A Look in the Mirror

- Identify the mask(s) that you wear in your life.

> **Why do you think you wear these masks?**

*What would it cost you to take off your masks?
Do you think removing the masks will be worth
that cost? Why or why not?*

A CLOSET PRAYER

Dear Father,

*I don't want to hide from you or from the people you have placed
in my life. Please help me to identify the masks I hide behind, and
then give me the grace and strength to take them off and lay them
at your feet. In Jesus' name.*

Amen.

Chapter 4

Broken Relationships
and Disappointment

BROKEN RELATIONSHIPS: I WANT TO EXCHANGE
MY FAMILY FOR A NEW ONE

As a woman who is both proud to be an American and also has one half of her kilt in Bonnie Scotland (yes, I tune into *Good Morning Scotland* on my computer every morning), I know how different the two cultures are. Scottish people are not very demonstrative or emotional, so I was quite surprised to discover how open and communicative many Americans are. But I have also discovered that just beneath the surface both quiet, reserved people and also exuberant, outgoing people are struggling with the very same things: broken relationships. They are one of the greatest consequences of the disastrous choices of Eden.

- Which relationships in your life come to mind when you hear the phrase "broken relationships"? List them here.

TROUBLE IN PARADISE

When Adam and Eve ate from the tree of the knowledge of good and evil, they discovered that they were evil. What a shock to those made in the perfect image of God to suddenly see that they were twisted and dark! Adam now saw Eve as flawed and weak, and Eve saw Adam as hostile and accusing. Talk about seeds for tension!

- What tension do you experience in your relationships? Give two or three specific examples.

We live in a world that is openly hostile to God and to his holiness. Television and newspapers offer limitless evidence of the enmity between the god of this world and our Father in heaven. At a more personal level, in our everyday conversations, we choose to use either the language of the redeemed or the language of the fallen.

- When have your broken relationships given you the opportunity to choose to offer the language of the fallen or the language of the redeemed? Give one or two recent examples.

- Which choice did you make—and why?

- If you chose the language of the fallen, were you trying to cover fear or shame? Explain why you couldn't be more open and honest.

I often think that I could be godly if it weren't for other people! You, too? That's why God offers us the power of the Holy Spirit, so that we can choose to live and love differently. After all, we—like Adam and Eve—have lost the ability to speak openly and honestly without our brokenness—without our fear and our anger, for instance—intervening. Our great hope lies in the fact that, in the power of God's Spirit, we can choose to communicate our fears, our hurts, and our anger with the kind of honesty that was natural for Adam and Eve when they were first in the garden.

"I AM SORRY"

I'm not sure that these three words come easily to anyone, but I've learned that they're a key to peace in many relationships. When I make a *wrong* decision that hurts someone, of course I need to apologize and ask forgiveness. But when I make a decision I believe is *right* and it hurts someone, I don't necessarily need to change that decision. I can say to my friend, however, how sorry I am that my decision hurt her, that hurting her had never been my intention, and that I love her. I can stand by what I believe to be right but still care about the impact I have on another person—whether that person's reaction makes sense to me or not.

- "I'm sorry I made a decision that hurt you. I love you, and I never wanted to hurt you." Who in your life might appreciate hearing these words from you? They could be key to mending a broken relationship.

Read 1 Corinthians 13:4–7 below.

Love suffers long and is kind; love does not envy; love does not parade itself, is not puffed up; does not behave rudely, does not seek its own, is not provoked, thinks no evil; does not rejoice in iniquity, but rejoices in the truth; bears all things, believes all things, hopes all things, endures all things. (NKJV)

What phrase suggests to you an approach toward mending one of the broken relationships you listed at the beginning of this chapter? Prayerfully consider taking a step in that direction.

A LOOK IN THE MIRROR

- As you look at your closest relationships, in which one or two do you see the most tension?

- What do you think the existence of that tension reveals about you? And what course of action in the relationship does that personal insight suggest?

> **What would enable you to choose the language of the redeemed instead of the language of the fallen? Be specific and practical in your suggestions.**

A Closet Prayer

Father God,

I ask you to pour out your grace and mercy on me—and on all my relationships. Also, please teach me to bring my anger and fear to you so that my words to others will be characterized by grace, compassion, and love.

Amen.

DISAPPOINTMENT: I DON'T KNOW WHAT HAPPENED TO MY DREAMS

No matter how well we think we know someone, we can never know that person's full story. Sometimes their responses to us can have roots in past disappointment, and disappointment can easily become bitterness. That's why God invites us to bring our disappointment out of the closet and expose it to the light of his love and grace—before we are consumed with bitterness.

Meet Abigail

I wonder how long it took Abigail to realize that her husband, Nabal, was an evil, cruel, and callous man (1 Samuel 25). How disappointing it must have been to realize that she was tied for the rest of her life to a man who was brutal and stupid. As we look at Abigail's story, we will understand how to position our lives when disappointment floods our hearts.

- What disappointments have you encountered in your life?

- Which disappointment is most crushing—and why?

- What are you doing to cope with that disappointment? If you're not pleased with your strategy, maybe Abigail can help. Keep reading.

"Why, Lord?"

Anne was long haunted by the abortion she had had in college, but she found cleansing and freedom when she later gave her life to Christ. Shortly thereafter, she learned she was infected with HIV.

> ***What events in your life, in the life of someone
> you know, or in the pages of the newspaper have
> prompted you to cry out, "Why, Lord?"***

- *Nave's Topical Bible Index* defines disappointment as "the
  non-fulfillment of one's hopes." What other sources of
  disappointment come to mind as you read this definition?

Disappointment hits at the very core of who we are. It rips at our
dreams, our hopes, and our very vision of what makes life worth living. So we acknowledge our disappointment—not to wallow in it
and have a pity party for ourselves, but to bring it into the light of
God's love and redeeming power.

A Way out of the Closet of
Disappointment

Let's look again at Abigail. Her husband, Nabal, had declined King
David's request for provisions for his army—despite the fact that
David had earlier protected Nabal's shepherds and livestock. Furious,
David vowed to kill Nabal and rallied four hundred of his men. But
Abigail heard about her husband's deed and immediately got busy
preparing a peace offering of bountiful food (1 Samuel 25:18). Then
she headed out to intercept David.

- Read Abigail's words in 1 Samuel 25:24–31. What about Abigail in this scene impresses you most? Also comment on the wisdom and godliness of her words to the king.

In your own words, state what Abigail did with her disappointment and what lesson you can learn from her example.

Here's what I glean from Abigail's life: She must have been very disappointed when she realized what kind of man her husband was, but she didn't let Nabal determine who *she* was. Abigail held onto God and to the integrity of her own character. God gave her both the grace to stay with Nabal and the strength to remain true to herself.

What further lesson on dealing with disappointment do you find in these thoughts on Abigail's story?

There are many modern "Abigails." You may live in a very difficult and disappointing situation, but when you throw yourself at the foot of God's throne, he mercifully gives you the grace to remain strong and true.

A Look in the Mirror

- Summarize how Abigail dealt with the disappointment she knew.

- What lesson from Abigail's life will you apply to your own life? Be specific about what you will do.

- What hope for joy after disappointment do you find in Abigail's story and, more importantly, in God's character?

A Closet Prayer

Father God,

I confess to you what you already know—the disappointment I feel in my heart. Many things that have happened in my life and in the lives of others just don't make sense to me. I ask for your grace. Please help me bring my disappointment out of the closet and into your healing and hope-filled light. In Jesus' name.

Amen.

Part Two:

Spring Cleaning My Life

Chapter 5

Facing the Truth and Taking the Trash Out

FACING THE TRUTH: TAKING A FEARLESS LOOK IN MY CLOSET

When my father-in-law, William, decided to sell his house and move in permanently with us after his wife died, we were thrilled. We also faced the task of cleaning out all the stuff he and his wife had accumulated during the forty-three years they lived in their house, and the attic proved to be the greatest challenge of all. When we finally had everything out, William said, "I forgot all that was in there."

That's the way it goes, isn't it? We push things to the back and mean to deal with them when we have some spare time, but—if you are anything like me—the spare time never seems to arrive.

WHAT'S IN YOUR CLOSET?

If we honestly want to get rid of any junk in the closets of our souls, we can only do it with the help and illumination of the Holy Spirit. And the psalmist, David, left us with wonderful instructions as to where to begin.

> *Read Psalm 139:23–24. You might even look at a couple of different translations. List two or three phrases that are especially meaningful to you as you consider spring cleaning your life.*

Before you get to work, ask God to show you what is in your heart, to reveal any fear that torments you, to expose any sin so that you can bring it to the Cross and be made clean and whole, and to help you let go of any unforgiveness, bitterness, or disappointment you're holding onto tightly. Ask God to fill you with his Holy Spirit so that you may honor him in all you do, including this housekeeping task.

WHY BOTHER?

Why bother digging up old stuff? Why go searching through your internal closet when life is going well? In a minute we'll talk about why we must deal with sin, but what about old childhood wounds and the wrong messages that are scripted into your heart? Can't you just live with those things? Absolutely you can. I don't believe that the Lord forces us to deal with things that we don't want to deal with.

- What encouragement and/or challenge does God seem to be offering you in this opening paragraph? Be specific.

"When the pain of remaining the same becomes greater than the pain of change, then you will change." What, if anything, does this anonymous quote mean to you today?

My sister, Frances, sees no need to go raking up things from the past, and I understand and support that. But I reached a point where I was sure that taking a fearless look at my life couldn't be any worse than living the way I was living.

Are you, right now, like Frances and see no need to dig up what is past? Or are you, as I was several years ago, thinking that looking honestly at your past can't be any worse than continuing on your current path? Explain your position.

Even if you're more like Frances, keep reading. I won't push you any further than you want to go, but some light spring cleaning will still be helpful. However, if you find yourself feeling the way I once felt, pray this prayer that had an intense impact on my life: "Father, I don't know what is wrong with me, but I am exhausted. I'm tired in my body and sick at heart. I don't know what to do. Will you please help me? Amen."

I had tried to fix myself for so long, and I had run out of options. Sometimes that's the best place to be.

"I Quit!"

When our son, Christian, was given a baseball autographed by everyone on the local Frisco Roughriders team, he was over the moon. He asked if we could go to the team store and buy a plastic display case for his new prized possession. After we purchased it, Christian tried for twenty minutes to open it and then finally said, "I quit!" I took the case from him and pulled the top off of it. It was very simple when you knew how to do it, but maddeningly complex if you didn't.

- What, if anything, does this scene say to you about your efforts to fix your life and to whom you might turn for help? Be specific.

I struggled in my own power for years trying to rid myself of fear and shame, of anger and isolation, but it was only when I finally said, "I quit!" that God began to do what he had been longing to do all along.

A Look in the Mirror

- As you consider your life today, will you choose to stay the same, or do you want God to expose the things that might be holding you back from experiencing the freedom and joy that are available to you?

- Whatever you answer, what does it feel like to live under a heavy load of past guilt and shame?

What is the hardest truth about yourself that you may need—and choose—to face during your spring-cleaning efforts? If you're not sure, don't worry. By the power of his Holy Spirit, God will both show you that truth and also help you deal with it.

A CLOSET PRAYER

Father God,

I pray with your servant David, "Search me, O God, and know my heart; Try me, and know my anxieties; And see if there is any wicked way in me, And lead me in the way everlasting" (Psalm 139:23–24 NKJV).

Amen.

TAKING THE TRASH OUT: BRINGING MY STUFF TO JESUS

I love fresh flowers. Even as a student in London with very little discretionary income, I set aside enough money for fresh flowers every week. (If I had to skip dinner one evening to afford them, I would gladly do it.) My favorite flowers are tulips, and I think a crystal vase with fresh white tulips is a work of art—pure, elegant, and simple.

A SINGLE WHITE FLOWER

A young woman had spent years on the streets of London as a prostitute. One night a female Salvation Army officer approached her and gave her a single white flower. As this broken woman held the flower in her hand, she wept and confessed her desire to be pure again. The gift actually changed her life.

In the Gospel of Luke we see "a certain woman who was a sinner" so touched by Christ that she, too, turns her life around.

> *Read Luke 7:36–38 and then verses 11–17.*
> *What do you think prompted this prostitute to*
> *push her way through a party of judgmental,*
> *religious folks to get to the feet of Jesus?*

> *Consider the culture of her time as well as the*
> *party she crashed. What risks did this desperate*
> *woman take?*

I see in this precious woman a person who has reached the point of knowing that the pain of change could not be worse than the pain she was living with.

GRIEF AND THE WASHING OF FEET

The woman—known only as a sinner—wept such tears of grief and repentance that she was able to wash the feet of Jesus with them.

- Read Luke 7:44. Jesus pointed out that this woman's sins were great. But what other great attributes did her humble act reveal?

This woman's repentance was genuine, and her love for Jesus, her Savior, was great. She gave Jesus the opportunity to teach Simon, the host, as well as each one of us how we are to view our sins. Jesus tells a story about two men who owed money to a bank, one five hundred coins and one fifty. The bank manager decided to forgive both debts. Which debtor, Jesus asked, would be more grateful?

> *Read Luke 7:43–47. Which debtor would be more grateful—and why?*

- Now, honestly consider whether you are more like Simon or the woman who washed Jesus' feet. Explain the similarity.

As I saw it (until I found myself sitting in a little church beside the psychiatric nurse who had accompanied me), I wasn't one of the big sinners. What I totally missed was that all the sin I had shoved into the back of my closet—the shame, unforgiveness, and anger— were just as potent as those sins that are more obvious.

- When, if ever, have you seen the blackness in your own heart—the self-righteousness, pride, self-pity, and/or shame? What prompted that realization?

- When, if ever, have you known that you needed Jesus to save you from your sins—and that he was waiting for you? What did you do with that insight?

I was once proud that I had never engaged in sexual sin, but my thought life was not always pure. I was proud that I had never physically harmed anyone, but my anger had stabbed people in the heart. I was proud that I had never been addicted to drugs or alcohol, but I had abused food and used it to cover my pain. As I began to bring my trash out of the closet, I wept.

- What are you hiding? What serves as a barrier between you and God? (Alcohol, pain medication, adultery, impure thoughts, bitterness, unforgiveness, self-righteousness, etc.?)

If you will bring whatever you are hiding to the foot of the Cross, Jesus will take it all and, in return, give you a new heart and a clean spirit.

A Look in the Mirror

- What sin do you struggle with most?

- Are you willing to take the trash out? Why or why not?

A Closet Prayer

Father God,

I confess that I am a sinner. Please give me the grace to see the familiar and specific sins that I am blind to and then help me take them to the foot of the Cross. Help me receive from you a new heart and a clean spirit.

Amen.

Chapter 6

Timing Is Everything
and Returning What Doesn't Fit

TIMING IS EVERYTHING:
RELEASING CHILDHOOD PAIN

In August 2004 Barry, Christian, Belle (our Bichon Frise pup), and I moved from Nashville, Tennessee, to Dallas, Texas. The exhaustion of the whole relocation was overwhelming, and a head-on collision with a driver who was high released the floodgates. After he yelled, "Listen ____, if you don't want more trouble you'd better get back in your __ car and get the ____ out of here!" I pulled into a parking lot and cried and cried. The scorpion I encountered in our new home on our second night was the icing on the cake.

THE GIFT

Being in Dallas meant finding a new psychiatrist, so I made an appointment with Dr. Paul Meier—whom I had interviewed a couple of times on *The 700 Club*. Dr. Meier asked me, "When your father felt that uncontrollable rage coming on, did he take it out on all three children?" The answer to this question was stored in the darkest corner of my closet. It had never made sense to me that Dad took his anger out only on me. Then Dr. Meier explained that when someone has had part of his brain destroyed and doesn't know what to do with his thoughts and emotions inside, he hits the one person he believes will still love him, no matter what. "Your dad wasn't telling you that he didn't love you. He was telling you how much he did love you in the only way he knew how."

• What encouragement to take out your trash do you find in this scene from my life?

The brain is such a complicated instrument. Like a computer, it records information and saves it to the hard drive of the soul. But when my computer freezes or malfunctions, I can tell it to go back to the setting I had at an earlier date—and it will. Wouldn't it be wonderful if we could do the same with our brain—if we could erase any bad memory and restore the original factory settings?

We don't get to clean our hard drive, as it were, but we are invited to bring the broken pieces to the One who made us, and he will give us the grace to live with understanding and hope again.

• What "broken pieces" (memories, hurts, behaviors, sins, etc.) might you take to the Creator?

• Is the timing right for you to do just that? Why or why not? Choose to believe that God loves you greatly (because he does!), and then let his amazing love cast out any fear that you feel at the prospect of taking out the trash of your life (1 John 4:18a).

A New Beginning

Within the church there seem to exist two camps for dealing with painful memories: those who encourage counseling and therapy and those who believe that all a Christian has to remember is that she is a new creature in Christ, old things are passed away, and God has made everything new.

> *What value do you find in each camp's perspective?*

> *In which camp do you tend to find yourself? Why? What, if anything, makes you nervous about the other camp?*

I have set up my own little camp in between these two extremes, and I would love for you to join me.

- Read Psalm 23:2–4, and you'll learn a little about my camp. What phrases are especially appealing to you? Why?

THE LOAVES AND FISHES PRINCIPLE REVISITED

If we choose to remain locked in our pain, we are unable to help anyone else. If we refuse to face our pain and instead stuff it back into the depths of our closets, we are unable to truly connect with people. But when we face what has happened to us, bring it into the light, and allow the risen Christ to meet us there, miracles can happen.

- I marvel at the way our Father redeems our pain. When, for instance, have you seen someone powerfully proclaim God's goodness because of a painful experience in his or her life? Or when has someone related to you with compassion because that person, too, knows pain? Describe the situation.

- God your Father can redeem your pain and make it a point of strength, if not an avenue for ministry. And since he deals with all of us as individuals, I trust the Holy Spirit to give you wisdom to know what you should do. Right now, what sense—however vague—do you have of how God might want to use the pain you've experienced as a starting point for insightful and compassionate ministry?

If you feel stuck and don't know how to work through what you are dealing with, I encourage you to talk with a counselor, a pastor, or a Christian woman you respect—and get some help. Or, for help finding a counselor, call 1–800–NEWLIFE. This organization keeps a registry of reputable therapists, as does the Meier clinic at 1–888–7CLINIC. You can also check out several helpful links at my Web site, www.sheilawalsh.com.

OUR PAIN REDEEMED

The enemy of our souls would love for us to either remain in our pain without hope or to cover over the pain even if it is affecting how we live our lives. When we are able—by God's grace—to give the broken pieces to the Lord, to give him the loaves and fishes of our story, then Jesus will bless it, break it, and feed his people. You will be amazed at what God can do when you are willing to let him.

- Are you willing to let him? Why or why not? Make your willingness or your hesitation the focus of prayer right now.

A LOOK IN THE MIRROR

- What have you done to deal with the pain from your past? Be specific.

- What might God do to redeem the worst moments of your life? Let your imagination go. After all, he is able to do far greater than we can ask or imagine (Ephesians 3:20).

- Are you willing to allow God to open a door out of your pain? Why or why not?

A Closet Prayer

Father,

I thank you that even though I live in a broken world you, who can heal and redeem my brokenness, are always with me. I invite you by your Holy Spirit to open a door of healing for me and to guide my steps as I walk across that threshold. I ask you to help me receive the healing you want to give me and then please use my life to bring hope to others. For Jesus' sake and his glory.

Amen.

RETURNING WHAT DOESN'T FIT: I WILL NOT TAKE ON OTHER PEOPLE'S DREAMS OR OFFENSES

It is a wonderful thing to see someone find the path that is right for her. It can even make the most cynical and embittered soul rejoice, if only for a moment. (If you want a wonderful illustration of this truth, I recommend that you rent *The Sound of Music* and watch the story of Maria Von Trapp unfold.)

THE FREEDOM OF THE CROSS

Part of the freedom we have in Christ is in finding out what he has called us to do and then giving our whole hearts to it.

- As you reflect on your own life, do you feel free? Explain.

Hear the invitation Jesus extends to his followers: "Come to me, all of you who are tired and have heavy loads, and I will give you rest. Accept my teachings and learn from me . . . The teaching that I ask you to accept is easy; the load I give you to carry is light" (Matthew 11:28–30 NCV).

- What heavy burdens, if any, are you carrying? Why are you choosing to carry those burdens, or do you feel that you don't have a choice? Explain.

The ill-designed burdens we carry can be those we have imposed on ourselves or those others have asked us to carry. Part of my spring cleaning involved recognizing how much I was carrying on my shoulders that Jesus never asked me to pick up.

Would You Like Fries with that Mouse?

When a stray cat began calling our house home, my son dubbed him Thomas O'Malley. One day Thomas appeared on our porch with a huge gash down his back and was bleeding profusely. We took him to the vet, and I wondered if he would understand that the ordeal he would endure there was for his own good. I was not prepared for his grateful response that was soon to come.

From that day until he died, Thomas became the consummate gift-giver. Each morning when I opened the back door to give him some milk, there would be a decapitated offering on the mat, part of a mouse or bird. Occasionally I would get the head, too, as a special treat. There was no way to tell him that a simple purr would have been fine.

For much of my life, I was like Thomas in my relationship with God. Every morning I would drag my latest "gift" to him. It might be one more thing I was going to do for him, one more prayer group I was going to join, one more person to help, or one more task to undertake.

- Are you dragging gifts to God? Are you working hard to do one more thing for him, whether it's teaching a Sunday school class, helping a lost soul, taking on a committee at church, adding an element to your daily quiet time, or something else? Give evidence from your life supporting your answer, whether it's yes or no.

- Now consider this same situation from a different angle. Are you the woman whom everyone else counts on to be there because you always have been there in the past? Are you overworked and underpaid but still smiling, saying that you're doing it all for Jesus, even though you are silently grumbling in your heart? If you've been there but moved on, reflect on what gave you the strength to do so—and thank God! If you're there right now, why aren't you stepping down from some of these responsibilities?

I have been the smiling face and willing hands that cover a worn-out, disillusioned, weary soul. When I was in that place there was no real joy, and everything felt like an effort, an ill-fitting burden.

> ### Read Matthew 11:28–29 in your Bible and then look at Jesus' words:
>
> Are you tired? Worn out? Burned out on religion? Come to me. Get away with me and you'll recover your life. I'll show you how to take a real rest. Walk with me and work with me—watch how I do it. Learn the unforced rhythms of grace. I won't lay anything heavy or ill-fitting on you.
>
> ### What is especially appealing about our Lord's invitation here?

- This is a different version of the same passage you read above, Jesus' words about heavy burdens and the yoke he has for you. Why do you struggle to exchange your heavy and ill-fitting burdens for the yoke Jesus offers you? What, if anything, is keeping you from accepting his invitation? Let him know what that something is.

I wonder what percentage of God's family is wearing ill-fitting garments. Sometimes the weight we carry is not a burden we took up for ourselves to please God or others. Sometimes that burden is one we took up when someone we loved was greatly hurt—as the following story illustrates.

I Don't Trust Them Anymore

One day while I was taking calls on a radio interview program a caller said there was not a trustworthy believer in the body of Christ. When I asked her what had happened to hurt her so deeply, I discovered that it was not her own offense, but an offense she had witnessed against her mother. As a young girl she had watched her mom receive mistreatment by a few women in church. While it must have wounded the mom, it had permanently branded the daughter.

> *It is much harder to watch someone we love being hurt than to be hurt ourselves. And it is easy to become bitter, but it is deadly. Are you feeling the burden of an offense someone else received? If so, describe the offense.*

- And if so, are you becoming bitter? If you're not sure, ask someone close to you.

Life is too precious to waste by holding on to a grudge, no matter how justified. If you're holding on to a grudge, you're like a bird trapped in a cage, madly beating your wings against the bars.

Skandallon

One of the translations for "offense" is the word *skandallon*. This Greek word refers to a trap or device used to catch birds and small animals. And I want you to know that "offense" is one of the enemy's most potent tools. It has devastated many believers and kept them in bondage all their lives because they feel that someone has committed an offense against them—that they have been hurt and wronged.

Even if you are right, and even if there is justifiable cause for your feelings, if you let them take root deep in your heart, you have given the enemy a place to live.

- What place in your life, if any, have you provided as a camp for the enemy? Remember, he'll camp even on understandable and justifiable feelings of offense that we don't let go of.

- What evidence have you seen in your life or the lives of others that a grudge won't get better, no matter how long you nurse it? Be specific.

- So why do we find ourselves—and perhaps why are you— nursing a grudge?

At times we are uncomfortable with God because we don't understand what he is doing. Read Matthew 26:31. There Jesus uses the word *skandallon* as he tells the disciples that God's plan will be so offensive to Christ's followers that they will scatter like sheep.

- According to surrounding verses, what specific aspect of God's plan would the disciples find so offensive and hard to understand?

God knows that we do not always understand his ways and his thoughts. But we need to take even those times when we've been offended by his mysterious ways—times which can be seeds of bitterness—to the foot of the Cross so Jesus can set us free.

> *What mysterious workings of God in your life or in the life of someone you love have offended you? Be specific.*

> *What, if anything, keeps you from laying the times God has offended you at the foot of the Cross?*

I encourage you to let go of grudges against people, and even against God, and to lay them before Jesus so he can set you free.

A LOOK IN THE MIRROR

- As you look at your life, what areas feel like a burden to you?

- As you think about the various demands on you—your time and your energy—how many of those responsibilities are you doing through God's strength and how much are you handling—or trying to handle—in your own power?

- What does your answer to the previous question tell you about yourself?

A CLOSET PRAYER

Dear Father,

I am tired of trying to be Wonder Woman, but I am also afraid to let my human limitations and failings be seen. So I ask you to help me. Please show me where I have allowed offense to take root in my heart, and please give me the grace to bring those offenses to you. For Jesus' sake.

Amen.

Chapter 7

Altering My View, Getting Help, and Receiving God's Outfits for Me

ALTERING MY VIEW: I WILL CHANGE THE WAY I SEE MYSELF

If you had lived in Eden, you would never have asked, "How do I look in this?" because you would have known you were beautiful. And you would have praised God for the beauty and grace of every other woman you saw. You don't need me to tell you that we live in a very different place from this.

- For instance, clothes that are being promoted to our young girls by today's trendsetters and fashion designers are so far from the garments of Eden; they are garments of the Fall. What specific examples can you give to support this statement?

- Growing up in Ary, Scotland, I shared a room with my sister, Frances, and within those four walls I shed many tears, despising the image I saw in the mirror. If you have ever despised the image you've seen in the mirror, what false messages and unrealistic standards of our culture fueled that fire of hatred? When, if ever, did you come to see the falsity of the messages and impossibility of those standards?

What changed my life wasn't losing some weight or having my skin clear up. What changed my life was touching the hem of Jesus' garment.

- Read Luke 8:43–48. In this scene from Jesus' life, what do we learn about the woman who touched the hem of his garment?

- What did Jesus do for her?

When Jesus asked, "Who touched me?" he gave this woman an opportunity to tell her story out loud. We find such freedom when we share our story. When, if ever, have you told some or all of your story? Describe the freedom you experienced.

If you haven't ever told your story out loud, what is keeping you from doing so—and what will you do to overcome those obstacles?

If this long-outcast and desperate woman had chosen not to answer Jesus' question and had instead slipped away, she would have missed his beautiful salutation ("daughter"), his recognition of her faith, and his benediction to go in peace.

> *This woman's faith moved Jesus to stop on his way to the house of a wealthy, respected man and attend to the silent cry of a poor, hopeless woman. What encouragement do you find in this truth?*

I don't know what you see when you look in the mirror. If you see a duckling who is ugly inside or out, I invite you to do what I did in 1992 when I felt most unattractive and desperate: I reached out and touched the hem of Jesus' garment. And I've been telling my story out loud ever since.

A LOOK IN THE MIRROR

- If you were asked to describe yourself, what words would you use?

- When you look in a mirror, what do you see reflected back at you?

- What places in your heart and soul bleed? Be as specific as you can.

- Are you willing to reach out to Jesus and touch him? Why or why not?

A Closet Prayer

Father God,

When I look in my mirror, I see so many things that are wrong. I see ugliness outside, and I carry wounds inside. I ask you to give me the grace and strength to reach out and touch the edge of Jesus' garment. In his name.

Amen.

GETTING HELP: I WILL ALLOW OTHERS TO BRING HEALING TO MY LIFE

In case you haven't noticed, it can be hard to accept help from others if that's not how you're wired. Some people won't accept help from others because they think they don't need it—it's a pride issue. Other people won't accept help because they think they're not worth helping—almost a reverse-pride issue.

> ### Is it hard for you to accept help from others? Why or why not? Explain.

The truth is that we all need help from time to time. When we are open to allowing someone else to bring perspective and help, overcoming years of frustration and pain can then become a doable job.

SPRING CLEANING HELP

Many of us try to make changes in our lives—to no avail. We try over and over again, and yet we find ourselves back where we started. We need the input and sound guidance of those who are gifted with the ability to help others.

- Where could you go to find sound guidance from godly people?

- If you're not sure, who can you ask for suggestions?

It takes a certain amount of internal fortitude to be able to ask for help, and perhaps even more to receive it. It's only as we are freed from our shame, fear, insecurity, and anger that we reach a place where we're safe enough to ask for help without either dissolving into tears or rejecting the helper. So often we live such lonely lives, and we don't have to.

Help Me If You Can

One of the most humbling but liberating experiences in life is to ask for help in areas in which we think we should be competent.

Perhaps you didn't have a good mother, and you struggle in your parenting. Or maybe you need to ask someone—as I asked Marilyn Meberg, one of my fellow Women of Faith speakers—how to be a good friend. Or you may not have grown up with a healthy, godly model of marriage, and you wonder how to be a wife.

- What aspect of your life are you unsure about? Who could you ask for help? If you're not sure, ask God to show you whom to approach.

I admire women who have the grace to say that they don't know everything. I admire them because I have been there many times, and I know how hard it is to admit. Once we ask for help, however, it's up to us whether or not we take it. To make significant changes in our lives, we have to be willing to allow God to show us where we need help and let go of how we have previously defined ourselves.

I spoke with a woman who struggled to pray aloud in her small group. Even after I reassured her that praying aloud isn't a requirement and that God knows her heart, she insisted that she wanted to pray out loud. But when I asked her "How long have you been talking about this issue?" she said, "Oh, for years."

- What issue do you talk about wanting to change but have yet to make any real effort to change?

- What message to and/or about yourself do you find in your answer to the preceding question?

Talking about change is easier than changing. But there comes a point when we need to make a commitment to a new and healthier identity and choose freedom.

A LOOK IN THE MIRROR

- What areas in your life do you need help with? Be specific.

> *How does it make you feel when you admit you need help?*

- Are you willing to ask for help? Are you ready to ask for help? Why or why not?

• Are you ready to receive help? Why or why not?

A Closet Prayer

Father God,

Thank you that you have made me part of your family. What a privilege to be your child! And as your daughter, I ask you to show me where I need help and give me the grace and humility to ask for help from my sisters and brothers in Christ. In Jesus' name.

Amen.

RECEIVING GOD'S OUTFITS FOR ME: A DIVINE MAKEOVER

Have you ever had one of those "Eureka!" moments when something that was foggy suddenly becomes crystal clear? Those moments can come when we are waiting for them, or they can take us completely by surprise.

LESSONS AT SEA

On each of the three cruises that Women of Faith has hosted, I have learned something significant about God, about myself, and about others. On our 2005 cruise, for instance, I had the opportunity to talk with three struggling women. One was dealing with painful events in her childhood and her relationship with her father. One was suffering with depression after her husband had walked out and left her and their children. One was dealing with being single and a deep, familiar loneliness. As I was praying for these dear women, my

"Eureka!" moment came to me: we're in the wrong nest. That's why everything feels so wrong, that's why we don't like the reflection we see in the mirror, that's why we experience such intense loneliness at times. Like the ugly duckling, we were born in the wrong nest.

> **What does the fact that, as a child of God, you are in the wrong nest mean to you? Be specific.**

A PARABLE

The truth that we were born in the wrong nest is key to understanding why we don't like the reflection we see in the mirror and why we experience such intense loneliness at times. One day we will look in that sea of glass and discover that we are swans after all. But until then we struggle with our reflection, with our feathers, with our relationships, with our environment. We were made for more, and when we were displaced from Eden and turned out into this earth, there was no way we could ever feel at home.

- When have you felt that earth is not truly your home? Give a specific example.

- Closely related to that question is this one: When have you sensed that you were created for more than this world has to offer?

• Read Revelation 21:1–4. What "more" awaits those of us who call God our Father and Jesus our Savior and Lord?

A LOOK IN THE MIRROR

> *What do you believe God sees when he looks at you? Be specific. (See Song of Solomon 2:4 and Deuteronomy 33:12 to hear what God says.)*

• In what specific ways do you identify with the Ugly Duckling?

> *Why do you think that we can't make peace with who we are until we see Jesus face to face?*

A Closet Prayer

Father God,

Thank you that you sent a Redeemer into this world to cover my sin and restore my soul. I thank you that I can take shelter under his wings until I see you face to face.

Amen.

Part Three:

New Clothes for a Wonderful Woman

Chapter 8

A Straw Hat and a Strand of Pearls

A STRAW HAT: I WILL CHANGE THE WAY I THINK

How we think does affect how we live, and I think we often under-estimate the implications of this statement. If you think that you are a failure in some area of your life, it may be because your thought patterns are keeping you in a rut. What goes on under our straw hats—what goes on in our minds—affects everything about our lives.

- When have you seen someone's inaccurate thought patterns keep him or her in an unhealthy rut? Be specific.

- Which of your own thought patterns might be keeping you in an unhealthy rut? You might even want to ask someone who knows you well to help you answer this question.

You might not feel adequate for the position in which God has placed you, but your adequacy is not the issue. If God has called you to do a certain thing, he will give you everything you need to do it!

- Read Isaiah 30:21. What promise does God make in this verse?

- What does that promise say to you about the importance of whether or not we feel adequate for the situation in which God has placed us?

The time to worry is when you think you know exactly what you are doing and you think you can handle everything yourself. Such unreliable thought processes not only keep us from being able to do the job God has called us to do, but they keep us from being who God wants us to be.

- When has your confidence that you knew exactly what you were doing given you a real-life example of pride going before a fall?

- Describe a situation in which your unreliable and overly confident thought processes kept you from doing something God called you to do.

We need to live not by what other people think of us, but by who God says we are. Only God has a crystal-clear view of us. We see each other and ourselves through the distorted pieces of our own experience, our failings, our insecurities, and our jealousies. If we want to change the way we think, we need God's help.

> *Read Romans 12:2. According to this verse, what are your responsibilities in this transformation of your thinking? And what do those responsibilities look like in everyday life?*

> *What will God do for you in this partnership?*

- Evaluate how well you are meeting your responsibilities and which ways of the world you especially need to let go of.

- Now note any evidence in your life that God is clearly at work in transforming you and making you more like Christ. (Again, a trusted friend might help you answer this question.)

Lessons Learned in the Dark

My new friend, Jennifer Rothschild, joined us for eight Women of Faith conferences in 2005. When Jennifer was fifteen, she was diagnosed with a rare, degenerative eye disease that would eventually plunge her into a world of total darkness. But that world taught her one lesson I will never forget.

One day she mixed up her eyeliners and lip liners and emerged with black lips and flaming red eyes. She told our audience that if you are ever having a bad hair day, put eyeliner on your lips and lip liner on your eyes and not a soul in the world will notice your hair!

The real point of Jennifer's story was that she has only one mirror in which she can see herself, and that mirror is God's Word.

- When you look in a mirror, what do you see? What do your eyes gravitate toward? What are you especially critical of as you look at yourself? What recurring message(s) about your appearance play over and over in your head?

- Read a passage you've visited before in this study guide—Psalm 139:13–16. Turn also to Psalm 40:16–17 and Jeremiah 29:11. What comfort do you find in this truth about who you are?

When we become believers, our transition from the kingdom of darkness to the kingdom of light happens in an instant, but the transformation of our hearts and minds is a process that will take our lifetimes. We can choose to dwell on our culture's definition of real beauty, or we can find our worth in who God says we are.

ALWAYS ON MY MIND

The God of the universe, who holds everything together, who is sovereign over every ruler on the earth, is thinking about you.

- Sit with that truth for a while. What impact does—or could—this truth have on your answer to the "When you look in the mirror . . ." questions you just answered? Let your concerns pale in comparison to God's great love for you.

God's Word never changes. He always sees us as beautiful and amazing. The challenge we face is to keep the image of the woman God sees more prominent than the image of the woman we see with our human eyes.

What practical steps can you take to do just that—to keep God's image of you more prominent in your mind?

The new hat that God offers for our wardrobe represents our choice to put on his truth every time we look in our human mirror. If we are to live as wonderful women in this world, our call is to change how we think about ourselves. We are most in danger of thinking wrongly when our hearts are not fully engaged in our relationship with God. When we are not passionate in our life with him, we look for something else to give ourselves to. We will look at this more closely in just a minute.

A Look in the Mirror

- List three things you like about yourself and three things you know God likes about you.

- Despite these wonderful things about you, what is your most common negative thought about yourself?

- What statement from the Word of God can you use to counter that negative thought? Write out a verse from Scripture that will help you line up your heart with God's truth when you are tempted to fall back into old unhealthy patterns of thought.

A Closet Prayer

Father God,

Thank you that you are always thinking about me. Thank you that your thoughts toward me are always good and loving and merciful. How amazing those truths are! Help me, Father, to line my thoughts up with your Word, with truth about your love for me and my value to you. I pray in Jesus' name.

Amen.

A STRAND OF PEARLS: I WILL GUARD MY HEART

I believe that when God has our hearts, really has them, when there is nothing in life more important than serving and loving him, only then do we feel really alive. But many women today are bored with their lives. It's not a lack of activity that is the problem but a lack of passion. After all, busyness is not the same as passion. If we're merely busy, we can find our hearts engaged where they don't belong, or we can lose heart altogether.

- What, if anything, does this diagnosis say to you about your life? Are you merely busy? Are you passionate for God? Are you engaged in projects where you don't belong? Or have you lost heart altogether? Explain your answer.

Wherever your heart is right now, know that God has not left you alone in your circumstances. God is talking to you and me all the time if we have ears to hear him.

REVELATION!

I clearly heard God's voice as I recently studied Revelation 2 and 3. The issues Jesus addresses with each of the seven churches are issues of the heart. And I noticed that when the church he addresses is in a good place, it is because of their passion for Christ. When the church is in danger of sin, it is because their hearts have either become cold or are engaged elsewhere.

That is our story, isn't it? Even if we are separated from John's vision by two thousand years, the struggles and temptations that our brothers and sisters encountered then are with us still today.

FIRST LOVE LOST

According to Revelation 2:2–5a, believers at the church in Ephesus were busy with their activities, but they had lost their passion. Verse 7 tells us three steps that can change even the coldest of hearts:

Remember where you were and what first made you fall in love with God.

Change your heart by choosing to be vulnerable.

And do what you did when you first met Christ. (Did you devour your Bible, look for times to be alone with the Lord, and tell others about your love for him?)

- Have you lost your first love for God? Support your answer with evidence from your life.

- This week, which step of the three listed in verse 7 will you take toward recovering that love?

We can, by God's grace, rekindle our hearts to burn for him.

PURIFIED BY PAIN

Jesus warns the church at Smyrna of upcoming persecution, and he reminds them that those who endure will receive the crown of life. I find it interesting that, throughout church history, persecution has often been the strange friend of the believer.

Persecution comes in many forms. In some parts of the world, people die for their faith in Christ. But persecution can also be the relentless onslaught of chemotherapy or poverty or difficult relationships.

- According to this broader definition of persecution, what persecution have you experienced in life—or are you experiencing even now?

- When has persecution been a friend of yours? More specifically, when has persecution meant closer communion with the Lord, greater insight into who he is, and/or growth in your faith? In other words, when has your faith been purified by pain?

- When have you seen the faith of another person purified by pain and struggle? Comment on how God used that person's experience or example in your life.

The very things that could push us far away from God, when offered to him, can be the sweet ropes that tie us close to his heart.

THE DANGER OF CONCESSION

The next church the risen Christ addresses is the church in Pergamos. This body of believers had allowed some of the habits and practices of their culture to infiltrate their lives, even though these actions went contrary to God's Word. Some ate food that had been offered to idols, and some were involved in inappropriate sexual behavior—and, as we do today, they were justifying their behavior. Compromise can easily be confused with grace, but they are not the same. As our culture becomes increasingly tolerant, we Christians can easily be infected without even realizing it.

- Where might you be using the truth of God's grace as an excuse to be comfortable in areas where you should show caution, if not do a total about-face? Ask the Holy Spirit to reveal to you this truth about yourself.

- Having identified those areas, focus on just one. What are you saying to yourself to defend and justify your behavior? Now shoot holes in that defense. Doing so may help you find it easier to stop compromising your faith.

Don't settle, but press on for what God's best is. That is a pearl worth treasuring.

A City Set on a Hill

Christ commended the church at Thyatira for their patience and charity and their growth in faith and wisdom, but he complained about the mysterious character, Jezebel. Whatever the truth is about Jezebel (and there are differing views), the church is held responsible for her behavior.

- I believe the challenge to the church at Thyatira and to you and me is found in Jesus' teaching in Matthew 5:13–16. Read those verses. What is Jesus' charge in this passage?

- What are people seeing about Jesus from the way you live your life?

We are called to live in our culture with pure hearts, fully engaged in loving Jesus and sharing his grace and mercy at every possible opportunity.

A Long Obedience in the Same Direction

The apathetic church at Sardis was in a desperate situation—and apparently unaware of their precarious position. They had become tired and were simply going through the motions of their faith.

- Are you merely going through the motions of your faith? Explain.

- What charge did Paul issue believers in Galatians 6:9?

Walking faithfully with Christ year after year takes vigilant commitment. It's not easy to keep doing the right things over and over. It's no walk in the park to keep on loving, keep on forgiving, keep on serving, but that is what we are called to do as Christ's church.

YOU SHINE!

The church in Philadelphia—in contrast to her sister church in Sardis—had persevered. The believers in Philadelphia had remained faithful, and Jesus has nothing but praise for them. The message for them is to remember that Christ is coming back soon.

- Jesus is coming back! Into what specific situation in your life does that speak real hope?

Sometimes we need a bigger picture than our current expectations, don't we? So don't lose sight of who you are and where you are headed. In your own words or with the help of Scripture, state just who you are and exactly where you're headed.

When we lose sight of the bigger picture and become ensnared by the issues and loves of this world, we can find ourselves in the situation of this last church.

DON'T BELIEVE YOUR OWN PRESS

The church in Laodicia made God sick (see Revelation 3:16). Jesus said: "You say, 'I am rich, have become wealthy, and have need of nothing'—and do not know that you are wretched, miserable, poor, blind, and naked" (Revelation 3:17 NKJV). They had come to a place where they didn't even realize God was no longer in the picture of their lives.

- Who in your life could and would confront you if you drifted away from the Lord as the believers at Laodicia had? If you don't have anyone who would, make it a focus of prayer and energy to find someone.

The pervading spirit of Laodicia was like warm soup. And I have a pet peeve with soup that tastes like it's been sitting out for twenty minutes before being served. It represents a meal that has not been carefully watched over.

- Consider now your relationship with God and how well you're tending to it and keeping the fire beneath it stoked. If "10" is piping hot and "5" is Laodician warm soup, what temperature is your personal worship? Bible study? Efforts to serve God? Prayer time? What might you do to turn up the heat wherever you need to?

God wants our hearts fully engaged as we offer our lives to him. You'll know no joy in offering him less than the best. It blesses neither the giver nor the one who receives.

She Who Has an Ear to Hear, Let Her Hear

God wants our hearts. He doesn't want our activity alone, our busyness, our long list of things we have done for him. He wants us.

- What percentage of you—what percentage of your heart— does God have? And on what are you basing your answer?

- What keeps God from having more of you—and what can you do about those things? However good those things might be, they're keeping you from the better—from wholehearted devotion to your God.

God loves us, and it is his driving passion to be loved by us. You were made for nothing less. May the truth of these pearls wrap around your heart. You are a wonderful woman!

A Look in the Mirror

- As you reflect on your life, what things make your heart beat faster because you are passionate about them?

Which of the seven churches do you most relate to? Explain your choice.

What can you do to rekindle your first love for God?

A CLOSET PRAYER

Father God,

Thank you that you want more than my days, my efforts, my accomplishments. You want my heart. And I want to give you all of my heart, but I'm not exactly sure how to live that way. So I ask that, by the power of your Holy Spirit, you would rekindle— or light for the first time—a flame that burns for you and you alone. In Jesus' name.

Amen.

Chapter 9

A Chair in the Corner
and Running Shoes

A CHAIR IN THE CORNER:
I WILL NEVER BE GOOD ENOUGH

How much time do you spend alone? You may only find time to read a few lines of a devotional in your own private sanctuary (the one that flushes!). Or alone time might be the time you spend stuck in traffic. Or the very idea of having alone time may be totally laughable—if only you had enough strength to laugh.

- How much time do you spend alone in a typical day or a typical week? Why?

- Would you like to be able to spend more time alone—or does the prospect seem less than appealing or even threatening? Explain your answer.

We are not a culture that embraces solitude, but alone time was a high priority for Christ. He often walked away from people who still had needs, problems, and sicknesses so that he could be alone with his Father. If this was a priority for Jesus, we are foolish to ignore this pattern in his life, this example for ours.

A Prepared Life

I truly believe that one of the most important lessons I am learning at the moment is my need to spend alone time with God in the midst of my rushed life. Christ knew that it was in his times of quiet communion with his Father that he received the grace and strength for what was to come. And God offers the same to you and me.

- Think about your life for a moment. What are you anxious about? What thoughts typically run through your head as you rush from thing to thing? When was the last time you found a quiet spot to sit for a while and do nothing but enjoy being there (without falling asleep!)? Are you facing a dark and difficult time in your life?

It is not enough to simply remove activity from our existence. We have to replace it with something better. And what could be better than time with our heavenly Father?

- Read John 14:27, John 16:33, and Philippians 4:6–7. In the verses from John, what does Jesus want us to experience?

- What habits did Paul prescribe in Philippians 4:6–7?

- What do solitude and quiet have to do with receiving what Jesus wants us to experience and with doing what Paul prescribes?

SO FAR AWAY

- Does the peace that Christ promises and Paul wrote of seem a million miles away from the circumstances of your life today? If so, consider how you tend to feed your spirit.

Being alone and quiet in the presence of God is one of the greatest feasts you will ever experience. Spend some time with him as you think about this story:

I said to the man who stood at the gate of the year, "Give me a light that I may tread safely into the unknown."

And he replied, "Go into the darkness and put your hand into the hand of God. That shall be to you better than light and safer than a known way!" (Minnie Haskins)

Now find a passage of the Bible and some time with God as you think about its truths. You might start with Psalm 23, Philippians 2:1–11, or Romans 8:31–39.

A QUIET TIME TO READ

I enjoy studying. I love digging deep into a subject that I know very little about and gleaning from the wisdom of those whose lives' work have been to unpack its mysteries. I have discovered that study is a faithful friend if we learn its ways. And I've also seen that a great deal of damage is done, not by evil, but by ignorance.

• What does Jesus teach in John 8:32?

• Describe the extent of your knowledge of God's truth. What are your strengths? Your weaknesses? The areas you struggle most to understand? Your major unanswered questions?

Christ tells us that we will know the truth and the truth will set us free, but first we have to know the truth!

I like to take a passage of Scripture or a good Christian book and write down what strikes me or what questions come up as I read. When I get together with my friends, I'll throw these thoughts into the arena, and we'll wrestle with them to grasp hold of what God is saying to us. Why not try this for the next week or so? Even if you aren't able to discuss your ideas with friends, my guess is that you'll be blessed by what the Holy Spirit teaches you if you ask him.

You Are What You Eat

Each day we choose what we are going to feed our spirits, our souls, and our minds. When we feast on the news, the mail, phone calls we receive, or negative-thought patterns that keep recurring, we should not be surprised that fear, anxiety, and sadness show up in our lives. Our Father has an alternate menu for the child of God: a mainstay of hearty meals featuring the Word of God and seasoned with prayer.

According to the following verses, what does God offer us, his children, as sustenance for the day?

Breakfast: *Psalm 5:3*

                    Psalm 59:16

                    Psalm 90:14

Lunch: *Psalm 1:1–2*

                    Psalm 25:5

                    Psalm 71:8

Dinner: *Psalm 16:7*

                    Psalm 42:8

                    Psalm 119:55

                    Psalm 119:62

In the morning we petition, we sing our praises, and we are filled with the love of God! At noon we meditate on the Word of God; we choose to trust him and sing his praises. In the evening we thank God and rest in the promise that he is leading us. We sing and pray, remembering to honor him in all we do. And if we can't sleep, we get up and thank him again for his blessings. Sounds like a menu fit for the daughter of a King!

What can you do to adapt your menu to the King's?

A LOOK IN THE MIRROR

Why is it difficult to be quiet? And what can we do to make it easier?

- Where could you begin to carve some alone time into your day?

- What is your spiritual diet like every day?

A Closet Prayer

Father God,

Thank you that you sent Jesus to this earth to show me how to live. Teach me to be quiet and to feast on your love and grace every day, throughout the day. In Jesus' name.

Amen.

RUNNING SHOES: I WILL HONOR MY BODY

By the time Jesus sat down and began to teach, the crowd was large. He had traveled all over Syria, and as he moved from town to town teaching and healing people, many left their homes and followed him. They had never seen anything like this before. They experienced new emotions as they listened to this man talk and watched him gently interact with those who were bruised and broken by life. It seemed as if heaven had kissed earth.

Don't Worry, Be Happy

I wonder if any teaching of Christ is more difficult for a woman to follow than this: don't worry about the food or drink you need to live, or about the clothes you need for your body (Matthew 6:25–27). Boy, do we struggle with this!

- Think for a moment about the time you have lost and the money you have spent out of concern for what you are going to eat or not eat and what you are going to wear. I have wasted more time worrying about what I look like than on anything else. I could just slap myself with a large fish for being so foolish! Comment on how similar or different we are on this count.

When I was a young girl, I read a fashion magazine from America which prompted me to go stand on the town butcher's scale (neither my friend nor I had a scale at our houses). When I left the butcher's shop that day, I saw myself as I never had before. I saw myself as a fat girl, even though the previous day I had weighed the same amount and felt just fine about myself.

- Do you remember the first time you realized you didn't measure up to some standard of weight or appearance? Reflect on your experience—and look for the lies you believed or false values you accepted.

You name it, I've done it: Weight Watchers®, Jenny Craig®, LA Weight Loss®, Atkins™, Slim•Fast®, the Cabbage Soup diet . . . and on and on! I will spare you the blow-by-blow walk through my twenties, thirties, and forties and simply sum it all up with a comment my pastor made one day: "Sheila, if you just carried all your diet books up and down the stairs a few times, you wouldn't have a problem."

GOD HONORED HERE

I have realized for years that when I am consumed by how I look and what diet I am on or off, "God Honored Here" would not be an accurate description of me.

Explain how dieting and fashion can move you to make your body your own god.

- Can you join me in my very countercultural desire of wanting to honor God with all you do and all you are? Explain your answer—and what it suggests about the importance of clothes and diet.

As I prayed for God to free me from the compulsion to be so concerned about how I look, one phrase kept coming to me. It is the title of a book by Eugene Peterson that I read many years ago: *a long obedience in the same direction.* This phrase captures the heart of what it actually looks like to put on your running shoes and honor God in your body every day.

- On April 11, 2005, I started a healthy-eating program that included lean protein and good carbohydrates, such as fruits, vegetables, and whole grains. This plan is nothing original; in fact it's based on common knowledge of what our bodies need. How do your usual meals compare to this?

The first week I lost the most weight, which is to be expected. After that, some weeks I didn't lose much at all. But I didn't allow myself to dwell on being discouraged; I just kept going. A long obedience in the same direction! What can we do to just keep going when we're trying to eat healthier?

Even as I changed my eating habits, I had to decide what I really wanted to do with my body. Did I want to indulge it every time the mood hit me, or did I want to bring my desires under the lordship of Christ? Did I want a healthier body to serve him well for as long as I could? To tell you the truth, sometimes I just want to indulge myself and probably always will, but more than that, I want to honor God with my life.

- Do you want to indulge yourself every time you crave _____ (fill in the blank)? Or do you want to bring your desires under the lordship of Christ? Did you want a healthier body so you can serve God well for as long as possible?

- What might you do in addition to tweaking—or revamping—your diet so that you might have a healthier body? (Hint: A coach I know says, "Find something you like to do—and do it!")

Every day we have the opportunity to put on our running shoes. After all, the shoes don't just slip onto our feet by themselves! We have to bend down and put them on. Likewise, honoring the Lord with our bodies won't "just happen." We have to get up every day, mentally put on those shoes, and say, "Today, Lord, is one more day when I will take a long obedience in the same direction."

You can do it, wonderful woman!

A Look in the Mirror

- When especially has your body image dominated your thoughts? Why were you particularly susceptible then?

- Has weight or dress size become a god in your life? Whatever your answer, support it with evidence from your life.

> *Jesus said, "So I tell you, don't worry about the food or drink you need to live, or about the clothes you need for your body." What changes can you make in your life to let go of worry and stress?*

A Closet Prayer

Dear Father,

I want to honor you in my body and in my mind. Please help me to live a long obedience in the same direction. In Jesus' name.

Amen.

Chapter 10

High Heels, Flip-Flops, and Regular Hose

HIGH HEELS OR FLIP-FLOPS: I WILL CELEBRATE WHO GOD MADE ME

It started with a "Grow Your Own Frog" kit. We sent off for our tadpole, but Finnie lasted only a week. We graduated to a frog—with its own ten-gallon tank, UVA light, UVB light, and waterfall. Freddie did well . . . for several months. Then we went shopping for a leopard gecko because they're easy to handle, don't grow to eight feet, and are non-slimy. But at the pet store Barry, Christian, and I realized that we all love birds. That's how Grace, a very affectionate Jenday Conure, came to live with us.

WHO ARE YOU?

One of the greatest joys in life is finding out who God made you to be, with all the personality quirks included, and loving it.

- Think back to your childhood. What was it that made you unique and special? How were you different from your siblings? From your parents? What did you love to do at school? What were the things that you did better than anyone else?

> *What makes you unique and special today? Are you a high-heels gal or a total flip-flop woman? Do you love to wear dresses or only feel at home in jeans?*

When we lose the wonder of who are, we find ourselves trying to be like others because we are afraid to be different. But different is good!

There is no one else in the whole wide world like you. I'm sure you have heard that before, but do you truly understand how precious you are to God? I'm not just being rhetorical!

- Tell of a time when you were confident of God's love, of a friend's love, and/or of your lovability.

We are not always treasured on this earth. Our relationships with our parents or friends or spouses can lead us to believe that we may be unique but that our uniqueness is not a good thing.

- If you were to follow your heart and not be judged by anyone, what one thing would you love to do, have, or be?

- What's keeping you from doing, having, or being that? Is it really an insurmountable obstacle?

So often we are encouraged to blend in, not rock the boat, and not be different, but I say rock that boat and be who you are!

In his wonderful book *The Cure for the Common Life*, Max Lucado says that each one of us has what he calls a "sweet spot" where we are meant to live. He writes, "Stand at the intersection of your affections and successes and find your uniqueness."

- List your affections, and then list your successes. What uniqueness do you see revealed?

Read Romans 12:3–8 or 1 Corinthians 12:12–27. What do these passages teach about your value to the church? What commandments do you find there?

When you hold back who you really are, we all miss out. So whether you are a pet nut like me, a journaler like Luci Swindoll, or a wordsmith like Patsy Clairmont, whether you like high heels or flip-flops, be who *you* really are! You have a voice and a style that is all your own. It has been given to you by God so that through you a unique picture of our Father is revealed.

A LOOK IN THE MIRROR

- As you look back over your life, what personality traits that were obvious when you were a child have you suppressed as an adult? Is it time to let them surface again?

- Do you value how God has made you, or do you wish you were like someone else? Explain.

Earlier you worked to identify your "sweet spot." What might God be calling you to do in response to that insight? Put differently, what can you do to serve God and/or his people out of your unique strengths and gifts?

A CLOSET PRAYER

Father,

I thank you that you have made me unique. You have placed a one-of-a-kind combination of gifts and abilities in my life alone. Please help me—by the power of the Holy Spirit—to identify those gifts and abilities and then to offer them to you. In Jesus' name.

Amen.

REGULAR HOSE: I WILL LET GOD BE IN CONTROL

It was definitely an adventure in the lingerie department. I tried Spanx (they look like hose with feet cut off), I purchased a special tank top (it had a structure that would rival the Eiffel Tower), and I learned an important lesson. The control offered by lingerie is nothing more than an illusion. It helps the appearance of things that might have shifted, but it doesn't actually change anything. I also discovered that one of the best things about control hose is taking them off! It is such a huge relief. So, too, is it a relief when we take our hands off our life and accept the liberating truth that God is in control.

- What aspects of your life do you freely give over to God's control? Why?

- What aspects of your life do you struggle to let God be in control of? Why?

No Illusion

God is in control no matter how things appear. I used to feel at the mercy of circumstances or the whims of others, but now I understand in the deepest place in my spirit that God is in control and that he loves me.

When I experienced a parting of the ways with someone who had handled my career for many years, I thought I'd never work in the Christian music world again. That was a terrible place to be.

- When have you experienced something similar in your life—in your ministry, church work, marriage, or workplace? Put differently, when have you encountered circumstances that made you wonder about God's loving control over your life? You may be there now.

> *Either God is in control all the time, or he is not. God is either sovereign, or he's not. Why can't it be both ways?*

Again, either God is in control all the time, or he is not. His timing is not always our timing, but he is never one moment too late or too early. We Christians often say that we understand that God's ways are not our ways and that his thoughts are not our thoughts, but we rarely unpack that truth. Let's do so now.

SHATTERED DREAMS

Think about Joseph. His story starts in Genesis 37.

- When Joseph was seventeen, he had two dreams. According to verses 8 and 10, what did these dreams mean?

- What did Joseph's brothers do to him in verse 28?

- What happened to Joseph's dream then?

- Sold to a wealthy Egyptian, Joseph soon gained the trust of his owner. Read Genesis 39:2–6. What happened to suggest that Joseph's dreams were finally beginning to come true?

- But what happened in verses 7–20?

- What happened to Joseph's dream then?

- For at least ten years, Joseph was either a slave or in jail. What kinds of ideas do you think crossed his mind? What questions do you think he might have had for God?

- What happened after Joseph was released from prison? (See Genesis 41:41.)

- What fulfillment of Joseph's dreams do you see in Genesis 42:6?

Two things about Joseph's story are very encouraging to me. First, it is clear that no human being can destroy what God has purposed. Second, while Joseph was in the waiting period of more than ten long years, God was preparing him to serve. And Joseph cooperated.

Joseph could have sat around in despair for years wondering where things went wrong, but he didn't. Instead, wherever he was, he used his God-given skills and abilities to serve the people around him.

> *In what current situation, if any, can you follow Joseph's example?*

God must have been pleased with Joseph's character and growth. From a headstrong teenager who didn't display much wisdom around his elders, he became a mature, wise, and honored man.

ARE YOU STUCK RIGHT NOW?

Take a moment to consider your present circumstances.

Are you confident that God has called you to something in particular and doing everything within your power to make it happen? Remember that God is not looking for exhausted servants who run around trying to be and do everything in the hopes of being recognized and fulfilled.

- What do Philippians 4:13 and 1 Peter 4:11 say to you?

Or have you lost heart? Perhaps you once believed that God had called you to a certain task but, as time has passed and life has taken a few unexpected left turns, you have simply given up. Loss of hope is a terrible place for a believer to be.

- What encouragement can you find in Romans 5:3–5?

Or perhaps neither of those situations quite fits you. Wherever you are in your life right now, read Genesis 50:20.

- When have you seen something intended for evil used by our sovereign God for your good? Be specific—and be encouraged!

How Do You Spell Relief?

One of the things I first noticed about Spanx is how great it is to take them off. What a relief! So, too, with the tight control we try to have on our lives. If we could grasp, by the power of the Holy Spirit, the Genesis 50:20 truth that Joseph embraced, think how it would change our lives.

Say the following truths out loud:
God is in control, not my husband.
God is in control, not my children or parents.
God is in control, not my doctor.
God is in control, not my boss.
God is in control, not a terrorist.
God is in control, not _____. (Fill in the blank.)

Read Psalm 121:1–8. Consider memorizing it and repeating this wonderful truth to yourself whenever you find yourself worrying about something.

No matter what is going on in your life right now, know that God loves you and he is in control, so you don't have to try to manage everything. Take those uncomfortable control-top hose off, and breathe a sigh of relief. You are a wonderful woman!

A Look in the Mirror

- Does your life feel out of control? Why or why not?

- What fears keep you from experiencing the peace of God that Paul wrote about to the church in Rome?

- Do you believe—if not intellectually, then by the way you are living—that someone else has interfered with, if not completely altered, God's plan for your life? Explain.

- Are you ready to believe that God is in control no matter what seems to be true? Why or why not?

A Closet Prayer

Father God,

I am so thankful that you are in control of all things at all times. Help me in my unbelief and fear. I want to always be choosing to trust you. Even in seasons of waiting, I want with all my heart to live for you rather than merely waiting for my life to change. In Jesus' name.

Amen.

What a Wonder!

"Do you know what my two favorite things about you are, Mom?" Christian asked me one day. "I like that you love your life, Mom, and I get to be in it." My son's comment touched me deeply. For many years I had just gotten through my life. It's really only in the last ten or twelve years that I have loved it and have felt so grateful to be alive.

- We are all on a journey in this life. We have no choice on that front, but we are either growing or shrinking inside. Which are you doing? Give evidence from your life.

- Are you thirsty? Are you tired of trying so hard in life?

If you answered yes to that last question, Jesus is inviting you to come and drink deeply of his love, his strength, his joy, and his peace.

A DESPERATE HOUSEWIFE

I have had the joy of watching God transform others from desperately striving Wonder Women to women at peace, wonderful women of God. I think of Susan. I'm going to ask you to do something I asked her to do after I had listened to her beat herself up for three years.

- Write down the messages you received as a child as well as memories of your childhood.

- Evaluate those messages. Were they messages of grace that taught you to extend grace to yourself? Or were you—like Susan—constantly told to do better, be better, perform better?

If you need messages of grace to replace the negative messages you learned all too well, that were reinforced as you were growing up, read the following passages and know that God is speaking to you.

. . . Yes, I have loved you with an everlasting love;
Therefore with lovingkindness I have drawn you.
    (Jeremiah 31:3 NKJV)

How precious also are Your thoughts to me, O God!
How great is the sum of them!
If I should count them, they would be more in number than
    the sand;
When I awake, I am still with You.
    (Psalm 139:17–18 NKJV)

I will be glad and rejoice in your love,
    because you saw my suffering;
    you knew my troubles.
You have not handed me over to my enemies
    but have set me in a safe place.
    (Psalm 31:7–8 NCV)

This is real love. It is not that we loved God, but that he loved
us and sent his Son as a sacrifice to take away our sins.
(1 John 4:10 NCV)

And I am convinced that nothing can ever separate us from
his love. Death can't, and life can't. The angels can't, and
the demons can't. Our fears for today, our worries about
tomorrow, and even the powers of hell can't keep God's love
away. Whether we are high above the sky or in the deepest
ocean, nothing in all creation will ever be able to separate us
from the love of God that is revealed in Christ Jesus our Lord.
(Romans 8:38–39 NLT)

Just as I encouraged Susan, I encourage you to turn to one of these
verses every time you feel overwhelmed or condemned. God's living
and active Word can transform you just as it transformed Susan.

The next time I saw Susan, I was truly moved by the change in
her countenance. She went on to tell me that, as weeks turned to
months, she realized that she felt a little different inside, not so desperate and intense. She also told me that she stopped trying to save
the world and started letting Jesus save her.

THE WHOLE POINT

And I think that's the whole point. You and I are not the good news—
Jesus is. You and I can't save ourselves or our families. Jesus does that.
We can spend the rest of our lives beating ourselves up for being
human or accept that Jesus loves and receives us in our humanity.

> *I think it's time for another "read this out loud"*
> *exercise: "I can't save myself or my family. Jesus*
> *does that. I don't need to beat myself up for being*
> *human. I can accept that Jesus loves me and*
> *receives me in all my human sin and weakness."*

God made us as women want to be treasured and adored, but it is very possible that you have never felt captivating. The absolute truth, however, is that Jesus sees you as captivating. Want evidence? Read Romans 5:8.

TIME TO DREAM AGAIN

In these pages I've been privileged to speak God's truth to you—the truth about how beautiful you are to him, about his great love for you, and about how passionately he loves you. Jesus truly is captivated by you. And there has never been a moment in your life when God didn't love you . . . not one moment.

Now take some time to respond to God's truth. In your own words, write your praise for who he is (loving, forgiving, etc.), your confession of failure to live in light of his love, your thanks for his many blessings, and your cries for help as you try to live as the wonderful woman you are!

A quick review of some wonderful-woman fundamentals:

- You don't have to save anyone. Just let Jesus continue to save you.
- God is in control, so you don't have to try to be.
- Nothing that will happen to you today or tomorrow has not passed through the loving hands of your Father in heaven.

- Which of these three truths speaks most powerfully to you right now? Explain.

You are not Wonder Woman—but, woman, you are wonderful!!

A Look in the Mirror

- What challenges found in these pages are potentially the most life-changing for you? Explain.

- What passage(s) from Scripture referred to, quoted, or studied in this study guide did you find especially meaningful? Tell us why.

> *One of the first questions I asked you back in chapter 1 was "What do you hope to get out of this study?" Now I ask you "What did you get out of this study?" Be specific.*

> **Why would you rather see yourself as wonderful than trying to be Wonder Woman?**

A Final Prayer

Father,

Thank you that you see me as I am, warts and all, and that you love me nevertheless. Thank you that, in your eyes, I am beautiful. Thank you that you treasure me. Today I choose—by your grace—to start living in light of that truth. Through the power of your Spirit, having been set free by the life and death of my Savior and Lord, Jesus Christ, I want to be the woman you created me to be. I know that, because of you and only because of you, I am a wonderful woman! In Jesus' name.

Amen.

THE COMPLETE WOMEN OF FAITH®
STUDY GUIDE SERIES

AMAZING FREEDOM

OVERCOMING FEAR

EXPERIENCING SPIRITUAL INTIMACY

CONTAGIOUS JOY

ADVENTUROUS PRAYER

RECEIVING GOD'S GOODNESS

GIVING GOD YOUR ALL

LIVING A LIFE OF BALANCE

MANAGING YOUR MOODS

CULTIVATING CONTENTMENT

DISCOVERING GOD'S WILL FOR YOUR LIFE

LIVING IN JESUS

FINDING GOD IN THE BROKEN PLACES

LIVING ABOVE WORRY AND STRESS

UNDERSTANDING PURPOSE

KNOWING GOD'S WORD

ENCOURAGING ONE ANOTHER

A LIFE OF WORSHIP

RECEIVING GOD'S LOVE

EMBRACING GOD'S DESIGN FOR YOUR LIFE

WOMEN OF FAITH™
STUDY GUIDE SERIES

To find these and other inspirational products visit your local Christian retailer.

www.thomasnelson.com

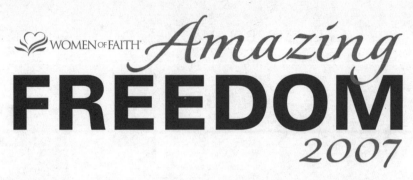

WOMEN OF FAITH *Amazing* FREEDOM 2007

"So if the Son makes you free, you will be truly free." – John 8:36

We often catch *GLIMPSES OF FREEDOM* but what about the *promise* of being truly free? That's *AMAZING!* Women of Faith...as always, *FRESH, FABULOUS,* and *FUN-LOVING!*

2007 Conference Schedule*

March 15 - 17 San Antonio, TX	July 13 - 14 Washington, DC	September 28 - 29 Houston, TX
April 13 - 14 Little Rock, AR	July 20 - 21 Chicago, IL	October 5 - 6 San Jose, CA
April 20 - 21 Des Moines, IA	July 27 - 28 Boston, MA	October 12 - 13 Portland, OR
April 27 - 28 Columbus, OH	August 3 - 4 Ft. Wayne, IN	October 19 - 20 St. Paul, MN
May 18 - 19 Billings, MT	August 10 - 11 Atlanta, GA	October 26 - 27 Charlotte, NC
June 1 - 2 Rochester, NY	August 17 - 18 Calgary, AB Canada	November 2 - 3 Oklahoma City, OK
June 8 - 9 Ft. Lauderdale, FL	August 24 - 25 Dallas, TX	November 9 - 10 Tampa, FL
June 15 - 16 St. Louis, MO	September 7 - 8 Anaheim, CA	November 16 - 17 Phoenix, AZ**
June 22 - 23 Cleveland, OH	September 14 - 15 Philadelphia, PA	**There will be no Pre-Conference in Phoenix.
June 29 - 30 Seattle, WA	September 21 - 22 Denver, CO	

FOR MORE INFORMATION CALL **888-49-FAITH**
OR VISIT **WOMENOFFAITH.COM**
*Dates, Time, Location and special guests are subject to change.
Women of Faith is a ministry division of Thomas Nelson Publishers.